I0800024

IMAGES
*of America*

# HISTORIC SAGINAW CLUB

This survey drawing shows the Saginaw Club and surrounding parking lots. The early lots were added to the initial property for hundreds of dollars, while the later additions were in the thousands. (Authors' collection.)

**On the Cover:** The East Saginaw Club is seen here in the early 1900s. (Courtesy of the Library of Congress.)

IMAGES
*of America*

# HISTORIC SAGINAW CLUB

Roberta Morey and John Morey

ARCADIA
PUBLISHING

ISBN 978-1-4671-0411-1

Published by Arcadia Publishing
Charleston, South Carolina

Printed in the United States of America

Library of Congress Control Number: 2019940804

For all general information, please contact Arcadia Publishing:
Telephone 843-853-2070
Fax 843-853-0044
E-mail sales@arcadiapublishing.com
For customer service and orders:
Toll-Free 1-888-313-2665

Visit us on the Internet at www.arcadiapublishing.com

*This book is dedicated to all current and former residents of the Saginaw area who love and appreciate local history.*

# Contents

# Acknowledgments

Members and former members who donated items and related memories of the Saginaw Club have been a valuable addition to this book. They are too numerous to list individually. We wish to thank the following people who were willing to share memorabilia and thoughts of their attendance at programs at the club. They are Ruth Braun, Nancy Seamon, the late Connie Harvey, Marilyn Dust, and Sandy Schwan from the Castle Museum. We also would be remiss if we did not thank the staff at the Saginaw Club, especially Cheryl Westphal and Laureen Lutenski. Our editor, Caroline Anderson, at Arcadia Publishing needs a big thank-you for keeping us on track.

# INTRODUCTION

At eight o'clock on Thursday evening, April 18, 1889, a group of citizens met in the common council room in the Schmitz Block in the city of East Saginaw for the purpose of organizing a social club. Oscar Wisner was called to the chair, and Ferd Ashley was chosen secretary of the meeting. The chairman stated the object of the meeting, and the secretary read the articles of association, which had been prepared. The club was organized with capital stock of $50,000, and the articles of association were drawn up and signed by 47 members. William B. Mershon moved that the board of managers be fixed at nine. The first nine members to the board of managers were Oscar F. Wisner, William F. Potter, B.F. Webster, William Callam, William B. Mershon, George B. Morley, Robert M. Randall, J. Will Grant, and John M. Brewer. The first officers were Oscar F. Wisner, president; William F. Potter, vice president; A.H. Comstock, treasurer; and Ferd A. Ashley, secretary. Of the nine members of the board of managers, three would serve for three years, three would serve for two years, and three would serve for one year.

A committee was selected to choose a suitable site for the clubhouse. Consideration was given to the present needs of the club and the growth of the city. The site chosen was 100 by 120 feet on the west side of Washington Avenue and north of Tuscola Street, offered by Herbert A. Forrest's bid of $5,000. After securing the deed and the title, a payment of $4,750 was made. William Callam moved that the plans presented by W.T. Cooper, architect of East Saginaw, be accepted subject to modifications and changes in the interior arrangements. The contract for the masonry went to William C. Mueller, and the carpentry went to Michael Winkler. The cost of the building, including the heating and lighting arrangements, was about $25,000. In 1890, the furnishings committee selected highest-grade furniture and equipment. The committee was also authorized to purchase four billiard tables. The building committee recommended three bowling alleys be constructed. A communication was received from Charles H. McOwber agreeing to grade and sod the clubhouse grounds at the rate of 1¢ per square foot.

The formal opening of the clubhouse was planned for May 29, 1890. Open from 2:00 p.m. to midnight, the club would offer a reception with music, a catered lunch, and dancing in the assembly hall in the evening. At the stockholders' meeting on April 8, 1890, it was determined that the membership be limited to 300, and the stock be sold for $100. If a member was to resign, his stock was canceled. The dues for resident members was fixed at $25 per year payable semiannually. Special members who were not city residents paid annual dues of $12.50 and had no stock in the club and did not vote.

Property at the rear of the club, measuring 35 by 60 feet, was purchased for $600 and the southern 20 feet was sold to H. Coleman for $200. Through the years, the club went through periods of prosperity and decline. One of the early club's most helpful members was Thomas A. Harvey. He was responsible for much of the club's advancement and increased popularity. In 1905, additional property was purchased at the rear of the clubhouse, and the building was enlarged at a cost of about $10,000, providing for a grill room on the main floor and a roof garden above.

In this and other improvements, Harvey subscribed liberally with others for additional stock to be issued. He also inaugurated the movement for the acquisition of art. The club is fortunate to possess a number of paintings that were acquired, from time to time, by gifts from prominent members. The large full-figure portrait of Shoppenagon the Indian, done by well-known Saginaw artist Eanger Irving Couse, is one of the club's treasures. A group of Western cowboy pictures was donated by Arthur Hill.

On January 5, 1893, Oscar Wisner died. The club presented a resolution concerning ex-president Wisner's death. It stated that it was largely due to his untiring endeavors and his interest in the welfare of the club that it was successfully organized and prospered. Another member of the first officers of the club passed away early. Ferd Ashley, the first secretary whose beautiful handwriting graced the pages of the East Saginaw Club minutes book, died in March 1895.

A communication was received from Joseph Fordney, president of the West Side Club, regarding holding a whist tournament. On March 7, 1900, the minutes noted that the Whist Club could use the club providing the steward could make at least $25 for the club. It was decided to invite the members of the West Side Club to join the East Saginaw Club. Up until this time, the East Side Club had been exclusively for members of East Saginaw. In November 1898, E.C. Mershon, William B. Mershon, and H.C. Potter Jr., and others presented Couse's painting *Medicine Man* to the club. In later years, when the club needed funds for improvements to the clubhouse, the painting was sold at auction for $250,000.

# *One*

# The East Saginaw Club

On April 18, 1889, a group of East Saginaw businessmen met with the purpose of organizing a social club. They were interested in having a place to relax after a day's work. They wanted to have their own building for a place to unwind and enjoy a game of billiards, a cigar, or a game of bowling. They were not to talk business, for that is what their motto professed: "Leave the burden of our toil outside the friendly door." The initial group of members purchased a certificate of stock for $100. The articles of association would expire 30 years from 1919.

A meeting of the subscribers to the stock for the purpose of organizing a social cub was held in the common council room of the East Saginaw City Hall on April 18, 1889. Ferd A. Ashley was the common council clerk and was called to be secretary of the initial meeting. (Authors' collection.)

Oscar F. Wisner, a lawyer with the firm of Wisner and Draper, was vice president of Hoyt Dry Goods and secretary of the James Stewart Company, wholesale grocers and lumbermen's supplies company. Wisner's law partner was C. Stuart Draper. Wisner, chairman of the organizational meeting of the East Saginaw Club, was chosen as the club's first president. This photograph, taken by William B. Mershon in 1890, is the only known image of Wisner, who is pictured sailing his boat *Zenobia* on Wildfowl Bay. (Courtesy of the Saginaw Club.)

The articles of association were recorded on May 1, 1889, with the State of Michigan. The document was signed by F.G. Egan, deputy secretary of state, with the seal of the State of Michigan affixed. The articles of association were signed by 47 members present. The document is included in the East Saginaw minutes book. (Courtesy of the Saginaw Club.)

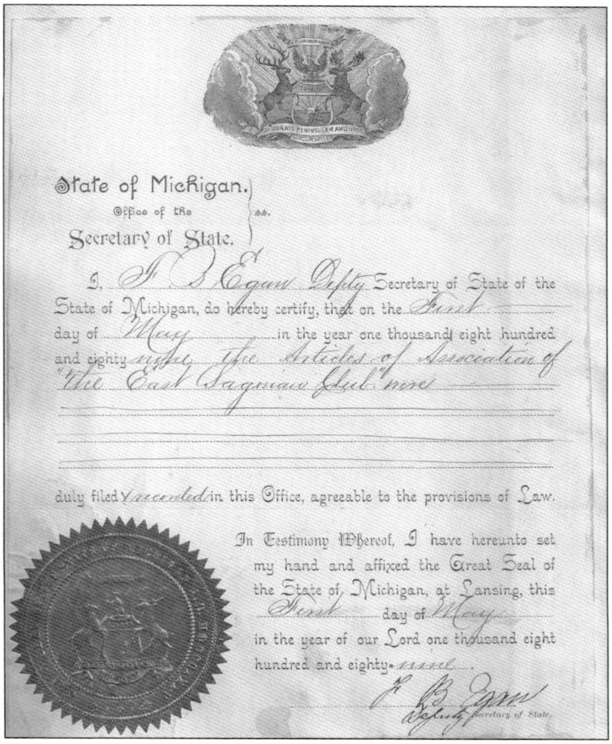

State of Michigan.
Office of the } ss.
Secretary of State.

I, F. S. Egan Deputy Secretary of State of the State of Michigan, do hereby certify, that on the First day of May in the year one thousand eight hundred and eighty nine the Articles of Association of "The East Saginaw Club" were

duly filed & recorded in this Office, agreeable to the provisions of Law.

In Testimony Whereof, I have hereunto set my hand and affixed the Great Seal of the State of Michigan, at Lansing, this First day of May in the year of our Lord one thousand eight hundred and eighty-nine.

F. B. Egan
Deputy Secretary of State.

William B. Mershon was present at the organizational meeting of the East Saginaw Club. He moved that the number of the board of managers be fixed at nine. After selecting the officers, it was determined that three members of the board of managers would initially serve for one year, three for two years, and three for three years. At each annual meeting, three new members would be elected for a period of three years. (Authors' collection.)

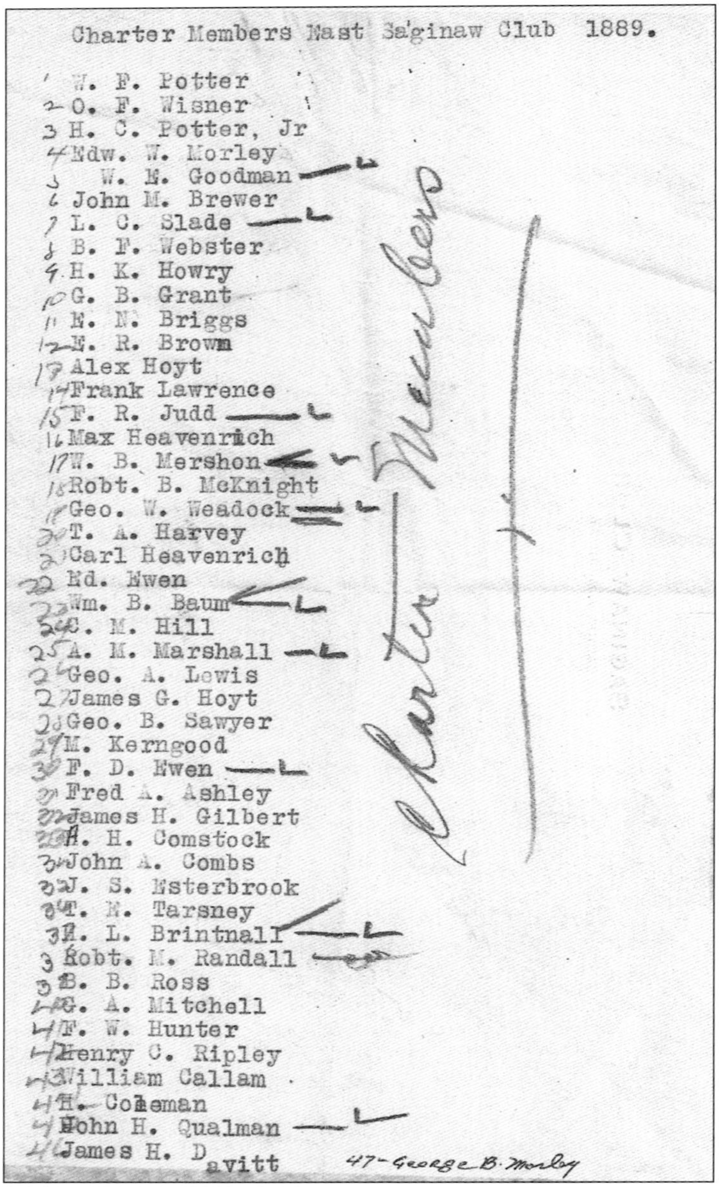

Charter Members East Saginaw Club 1889.

1 W. F. Potter
2 O. F. Wisner
3 H. C. Potter, Jr
4 Edw. W. Morley
5 W. E. Goodman
6 John M. Brewer
7 L. C. Slade
8 B. F. Webster
9 H. K. Howry
10 G. B. Grant
11 E. N. Briggs
12 E. R. Brown
13 Alex Hoyt
14 Frank Lawrence
15 F. R. Judd
16 Max Heavenrich
17 W. B. Mershon
18 Robt. B. McKnight
19 Geo. W. Weadock
20 T. A. Harvey
21 Carl Heavenrich
22 Ed. Ewen
23 Wm. B. Baum
24 C. M. Hill
25 A. M. Marshall
26 Geo. A. Lewis
27 James G. Hoyt
28 Geo. B. Sawyer
29 M. Kerngood
30 F. D. Ewen
31 Fred A. Ashley
32 James H. Gilbert
33 A. H. Comstock
34 John A. Combs
35 J. S. Esterbrook
36 T. E. Tarsney
37 H. L. Brintnall
38 Robt. M. Randall
39 B. B. Ross
40 G. A. Mitchell
41 F. W. Hunter
42 Henry C. Ripley
43 William Callam
44 H. Coleman
45 John H. Qualman
46 James H. Davitt

Charter Members

47-George B. Morley

This is the original list of charter members of the East Saginaw Club. This paper was pasted in a records book of the club and listed 47 men who signed the charter. As usual in most records of the club, initials were often used in place of first and middle names. The following are the names of the signers: W.F. Potter, O.F. Wisner, H.C. Potter Jr., E.W. Morley, George B. Morley, W.E. Goodman, John M. Brewer, L.C. Slade, B.F. Webster, H.K. Howry, G.B. Grant, E.N. Briggs, E.R. Brown, Alex Hoyt, Frank Lawrence, F.R. Judd, Max Heavenrich, W.B. Mershon, Robert B. McKnight, G.W. Weadock, Thomas A. Harvey, Carl Heavenrich, Edward Ewen, William B. Baum, C.M. Hill, A.M. Marshall, G.A. Lewis, James G. Hoyt, G.B. Sawyer, M. Kerngood, F.D. Ewen, Ferd A. Ashley, James H. Gilbert, A.H. Comstock, John A. Combs, J.S. Esterbrook, T.E. Tarsney, H.L. Brintnall, R.M. Randall, B.B. Ross, G.A. Mitchell, F.W. Hunter, Henry C. Ripley, William Callam, H. Coleman, James H. Davitt, and John H. Qualman. (Courtesy of the Saginaw Club.)

George Bidwell Morley was the East Saginaw Club's president in 1892. He was born in 1857 to John R. and Catherine Bidwell Morley in Painesville, Ohio. He moved to Saginaw in 1876 to work as a teller at Second National Bank. He became president of the bank in 1901 and chairman of the board in 1929. From 1910 to 1911, he was also president of the Saginaw Country Club. Along with his banking work, Morley helped found the sugar beet industry in Saginaw. After World War I, he played a part in organizing the former Welfare League. (Courtesy of the Saginaw Country Club.)

A group of prominent citizens and others gathered in front of the Saginaw Club in 1907 during the semicentennial celebration. Among those pictured in the first row amid other Saginaw people are Mayor Baum, Henry Potter, Ezra Rust, William S. Linton, and their wives. (Courtesy of the Saginaw Club.)

Thomas A. Harvey was one of the first Saginaw Club presidents. His term in office was in 1896. The club went through prosperity and decline, and Harvey was one of its most interested and helpful members. He inaugurated the movement for the acquisition of art. (Courtesy of the Harvey family.)

This painting, *The Venetian Boats*, was donated to the club by Thomas A. Harvey and George B. Morley. It hangs over the fireplace in the living room. It was purchased from the estate of the late Henry C. Potter and given in memory of Dr. Potter, one of the club's first members. Dr. Potter was an active and hearty supporter of the club and was beloved by its entire membership. (Courtesy of the Saginaw Club.)

Construction of the East Saginaw Club's building began using Jacobsville sandstone, a red stone primarily found in northern Upper Peninsula Michigan. Desired for its durability and aesthetics, it was used as an architectural building stone both locally and around the United States. The name was given in honor of Jacobsville, Michigan, a town known for its production of the sandstone. (Authors' collection.)

The red sandstone was extracted from 32 quarries throughout the Upper Peninsula between about 1870 and 1915. Shown here are workers with a large block of Jacobsville sandstone at a quarry of the Kerber-Jacobs Redstone Company at Portage Entry, Michigan. (Courtesy of the Castle Museum.)

An early newspaper article praised the East Saginaw Club building as a handsome structure that fronts on Washington Avenue. The cement walk and wide stone steps led to the entrance, flanked by stretches of green lawn. Pressing an electric button summoned a servant, who received visitors' card and admitted them. (Authors' collection.)

Entering the East Saginaw Club, visitors first encountered a tiled vestibule, which displayed richly ornamented art glass and a chandelier. The vestibule opened into the reception hall, which was 25 feet square, and a large area featuring a small front window, an old-fashioned fireplace with tile front, and a leather upholstered sofa of inviting proportions. (Authors' collection.)

George W. Weadock was president of the East Saginaw Club in 1905 and the first mayor of the consolidated Saginaws. His parents emigrated from Ireland to Ohio, where George was born in 1853. As a young man, he developed a strong interest in law. After his legal studies, he became one of Michigan's most noted attorneys. In 1906, he was thanked for making a valuable contribution to the art collection at the club. (Courtesy of the Saginaw Club.)

William B. Mershon, East Saginaw Club president in 1893, was a noted sportsman who traveled the country on his fishing and hunting trips. He was an early conservationist who watched the indiscriminate plunder of wildlife. He wrote two books: One dealt with the passenger pigeon and the other with outdoor life. One of his favorite projects was the establishment of the Lumberman's Memorial, which stands on the high bank of the Au Sable River. (Courtesy of the Saginaw Club.)

William B. Mershon's personal railroad hunting car, the "City of Saginaw," was used for an expedition to Dawson, North Dakota, in 1889. The private car traveled to the western United States by crossing on a ferry to Mackinaw. A variety of game birds hang from the side of Mershon's hunting train car. (Authors' collection.)

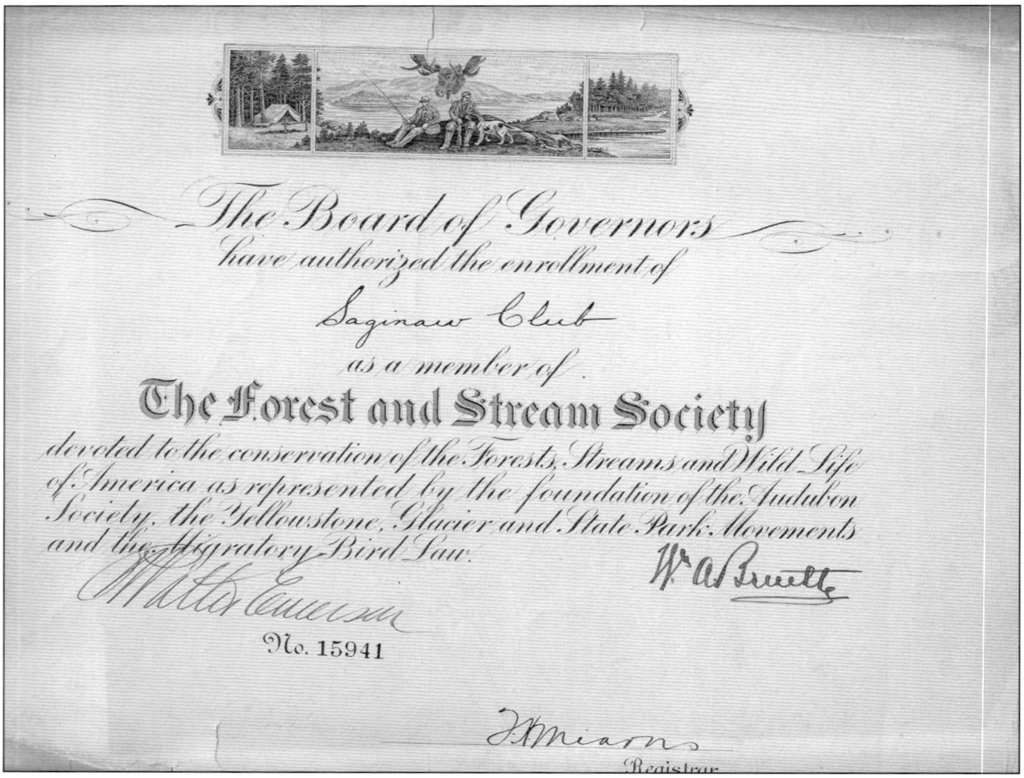

The Board of Governors
have authorized the enrollment of
Saginaw Club
as a member of
The Forest and Stream Society
devoted to the conservation of the Forests, Streams and Wild Life of America as represented by the foundation of the Audubon Society, the Yellowstone, Glacier and State Park Movements and the Migratory Bird Law.

No. 15941

Registrar

Through the efforts of William Mershon, the Saginaw Club became a member of the Forest and Stream Society. An avid outdoorsman, Mershon was infuriated with the relentless slaughter of wildlife. Mershon used his train car to go to Petoskey, Michigan, to witness law-breaking pigeon poachers. A Pottawatomie Indian, Chief Simon Pokagon, wrote in *Field and Stream* magazine that the passenger pigeon was an elegant bird in plumage and form. (Courtesy of the Saginaw Club.)

"We leave the burden of our toil outside the friendly door." This motto of the Saginaw Club is a reminder to members to come here to relax after a day's work and that the time for talking business is over. In the early years, the men came to enjoy a game of bowling, billiards, or cards at the end of their workday. (Courtesy of the Saginaw Club.)

In the early days of the East Saginaw Club, cigars were an important part of relaxing at the club. In fact, cigars were sold in the building and were always mentioned in income reports. Saginaw was an important producer of cigars, and some of these locally made products were sold at the club. (Authors' collection.)

Edward Wilcox Morley was born on February 9, 1839, in Lake County, Ohio. He received his early education there, and at age 18 went to Western Reserve College. In 1863, he came to Saginaw, and with his brother George W. Morley bought an interest in the hardware business of Anton Schmitz. The business was successful, and after two years, the brothers bought out Schmitz. The firm of Morley Brothers was formed in 1865 and became well-known in Michigan. (Courtesy of the Castle Museum.)

Edward W. Morley married Helen Frances Kelley in Chicago on October 9, 1871. They settled in Saginaw and lived in a comfortable house at 1330 South Jefferson Avenue. Here, they raised five children, Albert, Walter, Ralph, Abigail, and Paul. When Edward died in 1918, he was president of the Morley Brothers Corporation and the Saginaw Timber Company. (Courtesy of the Castle Museum.)

Harry Tuthill Wickes was the East Saginaw Club president twice, once from 1906 to 1907 and again in 1911. He began working in the business his father and uncle formed, and took over management of the company in the late 1890s. Under his leadership, the Wickes Boiler Company acquired many of Saginaw's most important and successful industries. Among these were coal and graphite companies. (Courtesy of the Saginaw Club.)

Yachting was one of Harry T. Wickes's favorite sports. He owned and sailed the 150-foot steam yacht *Capitola*, which was built to his order in 1904. The boat was used for many family vacations. In 1940, the *Capitola* was moored behind the Wickes Boiler plant when gale-force winds dropped the water level and capsized the yacht. (Authors' collection.)

These images from the book *Saginaw 1857–1907* show many buildings and businesses in early Saginaw. Shown here are the main-floor reception hall and stairs leading to the second floor of the East Saginaw Club. The eight-year-old clubhouse is pictured in 1907. Also pictured is the grill room. (Authors' collection.)

In 1887, architect Will Cooper submitted this watercolor perspective of the proposed East Saginaw Club clubhouse. The work was acquired through the estate of the architect Fred Beckbissinger, a partner of Cooper. The watercolor came to the Saginaw Club in 1963 and is displayed on a wall in the card room. (Courtesy of the Saginaw Club.)

Shoppenagon maintained the friendship and trust of many friends from Saginaw. Two of these friends were George L. Burrows and R.C. Morley. The men invited "Shop," as he was known, to be their dinner guest at the East Saginaw Club in January 1907. Shoppenagon was usually seen wearing a wool cap with stylized thunderbirds repeated around the crown. Attached to the top were owl and hawk feathers. (Authors' collection.)

This photograph is displayed in a prominent place at the Saginaw Club. It show Shoppenagon in his later years. He was proud of the two silver gorgets, which were typical of the ornaments traded to the Great Lakes Indians between 1760 and 1820. One is engraved with an eagle, and the other has an elaborate diamond design. Shop inherited these neck pieces from his father, and because his own son had died young, he willed them and other prized possessions to his good friend Lorenzo Burrows. (Courtesy of the Saginaw Club.)

The first book distributed to members of the East Saginaw Club in 1889 contained the constitution, bylaws, and house rules of the club. This original book was presented to the club in 1949 by Jean Stewart Walcott in memory of her father, member James Stewart. Along with the booklet was an invitation to the club lunch on October 4, 1890. (Courtesy of the Saginaw Club.)

Ferd Ashley, secretary of the East Saginaw Club, recorded the proposal for the purchase of property at the rear of the clubhouse. A.H. Comstock moved that the board of managers be authorized to purchase the 35-by-60-foot property at the rear of the club for $600. The proposal also authorized the sale of the southern 20 feet to H. Coleman for $200. (Authors' collection.)

Wallis Craig Smith, a businessman, was president of the board of education from 1919 to 1926. He was a member of the Saginaw Board of Trade, active in the Welfare League, and enjoyed playing a part in the Pit and Balcony productions. The local newspaper wrote that he was one of the most prominent men in Saginaw history. (Courtesy of the Saginaw Hall of Fame.)

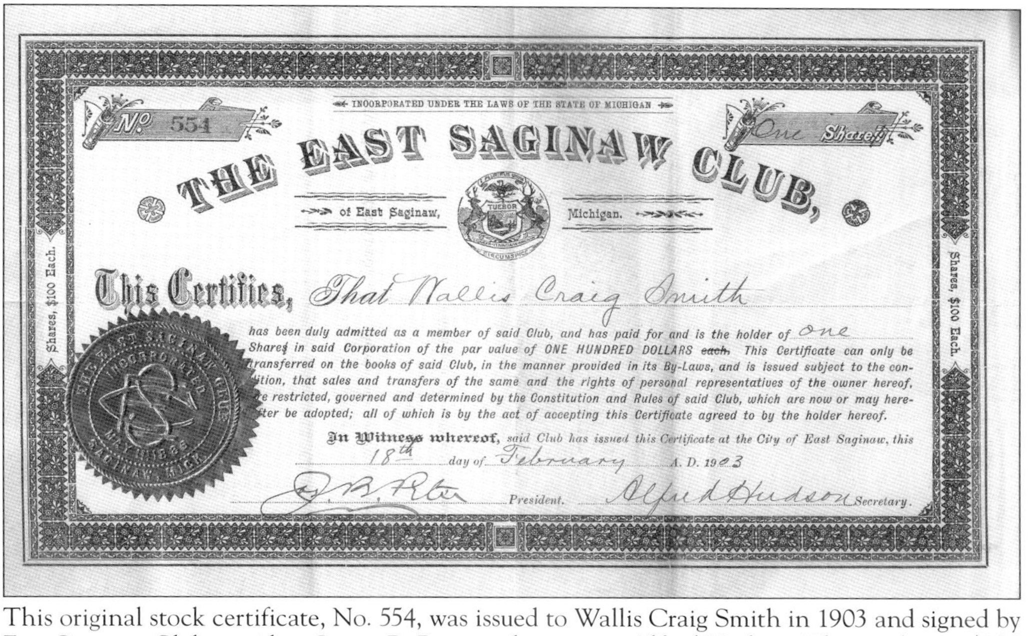

INCORPORATED UNDER THE LAWS OF THE STATE OF MICHIGAN

No. 554 — One Share

THE EAST SAGINAW CLUB,

of East Saginaw, Michigan.

Shares, $100 Each.

This Certifies, That Wallis Craig Smith has been duly admitted as a member of said Club, and has paid for and is the holder of One Shares in said Corporation of the par value of ONE HUNDRED DOLLARS ~~each~~. This Certificate can only be transferred on the books of said Club, in the manner provided in its By-Laws, and is issued subject to the condition, that sales and transfers of the same and the rights of personal representatives of the owner hereof, are restricted, governed and determined by the Constitution and Rules of said Club, which are now or may hereafter be adopted; all of which is by the act of accepting this Certificate agreed to by the holder hereof.

In Witness whereof, said Club has issued this Certificate at the City of East Saginaw, this 18th day of February A. D. 1903

J. B. Peter, President. Alfred Hudson, Secretary.

This original stock certificate, No. 554, was issued to Wallis Craig Smith in 1903 and signed by East Saginaw Club president James B. Peter and secretary Alfred Hudson. The stock cost $100 and admitted the bearer to membership in the club. (Courtesy of Ruth Braun.)

INCORPORATED UNDER THE LAWS OF THE STATE OF MICHIGAN

No. 720

One Shares

THE EAST SAGINAW CLUB,

of East Saginaw, Michigan.

Shares, $100 Each.

This Certifies, That W. H. Martin

has been duly admitted as a member of said Club, and has paid for and is the holder of One Share in said Corporation of the par value of ONE HUNDRED DOLLARS each. This Certificate can only be transferred on the books of said Club, in the manner provided in its By-Laws, and is issued subject to the condition, that sales and transfers of the same and the rights of personal representatives of the owner hereof, are restricted, governed and determined by the Constitution and Rules of said Club, which are now or may hereafter be adopted; all of which is by the act of accepting this Certificate agreed to by the holder hereof.

In Witness whereof, said Club has issued this Certificate at the City of East Saginaw, this 20th day of March A. D. 1907

H. T. Wickes President. H. A. Wolpert Secretary.

Stock certificate No. 720 was issued in 1907 to William H. Martin, a lawyer and circuit court commissioner. It was signed by Harry T. Wickes, president of Wickes Brothers, and Herman A. Wolpert, president of McCormick Coal Company. Wickes was president, and Wolpert was secretary of the East Saginaw Club. The cost of the certificate was $100 for one share and admitted the holder to membership in the club. (Courtesy of Ruth Braun.)

The booklet pictured here is the annual report of the East Saginaw Club given by retiring president Harry T. Wickes. Listed are the officers and members of the club. William H. Martin's name is included in the list of members. His stock certificate is dated 1907. This booklet indicates that the number of members was to be raised to 400. Credit was given to Thomas A. Harvey for his time and careful supervision of improvements at the club. (Courtesy of the Saginaw Club.)

An early East Saginaw Club member was Arthur Hill. He was president of Arthur Hill and Company Lumber and Pine Lands. As noted in the club's 1907 minutes, he donated three valuable paintings to the club. The minutes indicated that they were Western cowboy pictures. (Authors' collection.)

East Saginaw businessman Jacob Seligman was a member of the East Saginaw Club. Known as "Little Jake," he operated a clothing store on Genesee Avenue along with his own bank. Seligman's Bank of Commerce was located on Franklin Street. In 1899, the club's secretary read a letter from Seligman in which he stated that he could never live in Saginaw again owing to his health. On February 25, Seligman tendered his resignation as a member of the club and stated that he would surrender his certificate of stock. Harry T. Wickes stated that Seligman would be welcome at the club whenever he might be in Saginaw. (Authors' collection.)

Charles Kirke Eddy made his fortune in the lumber and salt industries. His family established the Eddy Family Memorial Trust, which supports many civic programs. C.K. Eddy died in 1900 as the result of injuries received in an accident. The East Saginaw Club noted in a resolution that his tragic death brought exceptional sorrow and regret to his many friends, associates, and relatives. He was a man of integrity and honesty in social and business life. (Courtesy of the Saginaw Club.)

As a boy, Clark Ring visited lumber camps owned by his father, Eleazer Ring. As an adult, he and Thomas Merrill formed the lumber business partnership of Ring and Merrill. Ring was also a leader in civic affairs. He played a part in the consolidation of Saginaw City and East Saginaw. He was a YMCA board member and helped with the fund drive for the new building on the corner of Ames and Michigan Avenues. He was a founder of the Saginaw Club and organizer of the Saginaw Country Club, where he enjoyed the new game called golf. (Courtesy of the Saginaw Country Club.)

Wellington R. Burt was a wealthy industrial baron. At his death in 1919, his estate was said to be between $40 and $90 million. He accumulated his wealth in lumber mills and lumber holdings and was also involved in iron mining, railroads, salt mines, and finances. He was the mayor of East Saginaw and a member of the Michigan senate. Burt's charitable giving to Saginaw during his lifetime included funding the city auditorium, the manual training school, a women's hospital, a Salvation Army, and a YWCA. (Authors' collection.)

The Burt Mansion was located on the corner of East Genesee Avenue and Cherry Street. In his later years, Burt lived alone with his servants in this towering three-story mansion. It was demolished to make way for a parking lot in 1959. (Authors' collection.)

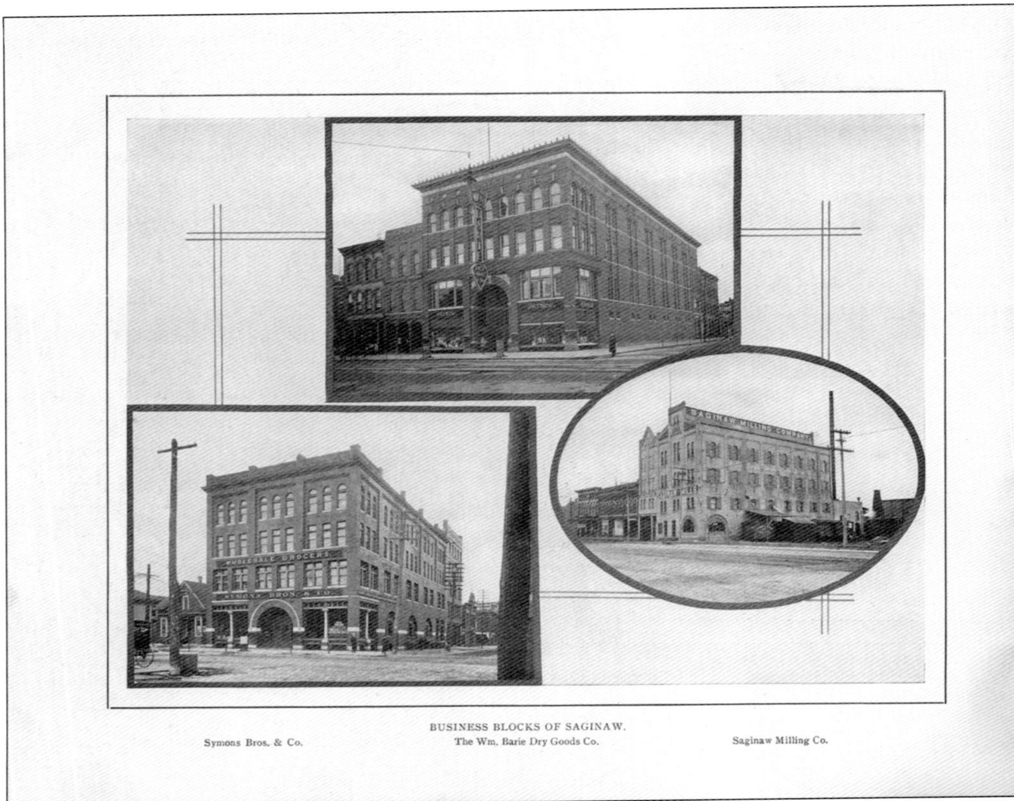


East Saginaw Club members William Barie, John Symons, and Walter Eddy spent their working hours at these well-known businesses. At top is the William Barie Dry Goods Store, which in later years became a Montgomery Ward store. At left is Symons Brothers Grocers, and at right is the Saginaw Milling Company. (Authors' collection.)

Henry Potter was born in Utica, New York, on January 14, 1823. He received a medical degree at Union College in Schenectady, New York, and married Sarah A. Farwell, daughter of a railroad contractor. He joined his father-in-law in the railroad business and became vice president of the Flint and Pere Marquette Railroad Company. Potter later became president of the Savings Bank of East Saginaw. He was a gracious host in his beautiful home at Jefferson and Holland Avenues. All four of his children predeceased him, as did his wife. Dr. Potter died in 1909. (Authors' collection.)

William S. Linton served in Michigan's legislature in 1890 and while there authored a bill that led to the consolidation of Saginaw City and East Saginaw. He was appointed postmaster of the east side post office, which he had designed after a French chateau. Linton was also instrumental in the development of city parks. (Authors' collection.)

Here, four Saginaw Club members enjoy time at a hunting cabin. Showing off their successful hunt are, from left to right, William Linton, Saginaw postmaster; John Baird, county road commissioner; John O'Keefe, attorney in the Bearinger Building; and H.A. Savage, president of Brady and Savage Inc. and American Cash Register Company. (Courtesy of the Castle Museum.)

Joseph Fordney was president of the West Side Club. He proposed holding a series of games of whist between the East Saginaw Club and the West Side Club. J.W. Fordney was elected to Congress in 1898 and served 12 consecutive terms. Because he promoted Michigan beans, the Senate serves Michigan bean soup to this day. In 1907, as a member of the East Saginaw Club, he suggested bean soup be on the menu there also. (Authors' collection.)

Aaron T. Bliss was a member of the board of managers of the East Saginaw Club in 1907. He came to Saginaw in 1865 and formed a lumber company with his brother. He was one of the organizers of the Citizen's National Bank, which became the Bank of Saginaw. Bliss was elected governor of Michigan in 1900. During his term of office, the Michigan Employment Institution for the Adult Blind was established in Saginaw. (Authors' collection.)

# *Two*

# ART IN THE CLUB

For the early members of the East Saginaw Club, an elegant building inside and out was a priority. Quality furnishings along with lovely and valuable art in all rooms was a must. Art was so important that, in 1906, an art fund committee was formed. It consisted of five members, Arthur Hill, R.M. Randall, E.C. Mershon, A.H. Morley, and Thomas A. Harvey. Many of the works of art were donated by the members, while others were purchased with members' contributions. Some of the artworks were so costly in the early days that more than 20 members contributed to the purchase. In 1911, Charles Willis Ward of Detroit and Eanger Irving Couse, the artist, presented the oil painting *Shoppenagon* to the club. Some of the artworks still hang in the club, while others have been sold at auction to support new projects.

Felix Ziem (1821–1911) painted *Santa Maria De Salute*. This framed oil on canvas is displayed in the second-floor sitting room. Ziem was born in the Burgundy region of France. He planned to be an architect, but after moving to Marseilles, he received some informal instruction in painting. (Courtesy of the Saginaw Club.)

A painting signed C. (or G.) Schumaker titled *Setter and Two Pointers on Point* is described in the East Saginaw Club minutes as "The Hunting Dogs." At the meeting of the board of managers in 1906, a resolution was passed to thank 23 members for their valuable contribution to the art collection. Among the donors were Thomas Harvey, Clark Ring, and Benton Hanchett. (Courtesy of the Saginaw Club.)

The Klikitat *Medicine Man* oil painting by Eanger Irving Couse was created in 1897 and purchased by the club by subscription. The asking price was $1,000. Edward Mershon, a close friend of Couse, negotiated for the club to pay $500. Couse was willing to donate the balance so that "an important example of my work should grace the walls of an institution in my native city." (Courtesy of the Saginaw Club.)

*The Grand Canal of Venice* was painted by Richard Day de Ribcowsky (1880–1936). Born in Bulgaria, he studied in Paris and in Florence, Italy, and is primarily associated with marine work. He came to the United States in 1910, traveled extensively, and settled in California in 1920. He died in Los Angeles. This work was presented to the club by Albert T. Ferrell on December 18, 1926. (Courtesy of the Saginaw Club.)

This untitled logging sled with horses was a gift of the artist, Leonard Meyer. This type of painting is made on top of a photograph reproduction mounted on board. The subject is a winter Michigan lumbering scene. It is dated 1962 and is oil on board. (Courtesy of the Saginaw Club.)

Leonard Meyer, the artist of this log train painting, donated this work to the Saginaw Club. The workers and the log train are typical of scenes of Michigan's lumber era. The date of this oil-on-board piece is estimated to be about 1962. (Courtesy of the Saginaw Club.)

*A Twilight Reverie*, featuring two men with pipes, is also known as "The Mortgage" and "His Legal Advisor." The piece was donated by the building committee in 1907. William Verplanck Birney (1850–1919) painted the oil-on-board picture in 1905. He was born in Cincinnati and studied at the Munich Academy, where he met fellow artist Louis Charles Moeller. (Courtesy of the Saginaw Club.)

*The Toast* by Louis Charles Moeller (1855–1930) hangs in the card room. Moeller, a native of New York, became one of America's foremost genre painters. A favorite subject was distinguished elderly men going about everyday activities in interior settings that reflected Victorian tastes. He attended classes at the National Academy of Design and studied in Munich before returning to New York, where he opened a studio. (Courtesy of the Saginaw Club.)

*View on the Cote d'Azu* by Lucien Potronat is an oil on board. It hangs in the second-floor meeting room of the club. Lucien Potronat (1889–1974) was a French painter best known for his depictions of picturesque villas set in the countryside of the French Riviera. (Courtesy of the Saginaw Club.)

This couple in black and white by an anonymous artist graces the wall of the second-floor meeting room. The man is using binoculars, and the woman is holding a drink. They may be attending a stage performance. The official title of the painting is unknown, and it was donated by a Saginaw Club member. The work is a facsimile of late 19th-century impressionist portraits. It was acquired in 1994. (Courtesy of the Saginaw Club.)

The East Saginaw Club minutes book of 1906 records the name of this painting as *The Wave*. It was also known as "Seascape" and "Breaking Waves" when it was appraised. The listed artist is A. Chester. Among the 21 donors of the work are Arthur Hill, Benton Hanchett, Ezra Rust, George Morley, E.C. Mershon, and other prominent members. (Courtesy of the Saginaw Club.)

This watercolor on paper, *Coming Ashore*, is another work by A. Chester. It depicts a Dutch seashore with returning boats. Chester, a 19th-century artist, was an active painter who lived in the United Kingdom. There is no information available on the donor of the painting, but the club minutes often thank members for adding to the art collection. (Courtesy of the Saginaw Club.)

*The Venetian Boats* by Andrew Fisher Bunner was acquired in 1910. Bunner (1841–1897) was born in New York City and is known for his landscapes and scenes of Venice. This work was purchased from the estate of Henry C. Potter and donated to the club by George B. Morley and Thomas A. Harvey in memory of Dr. Potter. (Courtesy of the Saginaw Club.)

*The Morning of the Hunt at Chantilly* by Jean Maxime Claude was a gift of Albert H. and Anna M. Morley in 1962. Claude (1824–1904) was a French artist born in Paris. Chantilly is a town 30 miles north of Paris where the Château de Chantilly hosts one of the largest art collections in France. (Courtesy of the Saginaw Club.)

*Chicago, the Mouth of the River* is on loan from the Saginaw Art Museum. It is a photolithograph on paper by the artists Frederick Schell and J. Hogan. Schell and Hogan had a partnership that lasted 30 years. Both were illustrators and lithographers and worked for the various Harper magazines. Of the two, Schell was better known. (Courtesy of the Saginaw Club.)

*Philadelphia, Girard Avenue Bridge* is by artists Schell and Hogan. Pictured is the first of three bridges that have carried Girard Avenue over the Schuylkill River. This first bridge was built in 1852–1855 and cost $267,000. The bridge was a three-span timber arched truss bridge. A horse-drawn trolley was added in 1859. Both Schell and Hogan were illustrators and lithographers. This work is a photolithograph on paper. (Courtesy of the Saginaw Club.)

This lithograph print of the oil-on-canvas work by Frederick Childe Hassam is titled *Winter Nightfall in the City*. Hassam was an American artist (1859–1935) noted for his urban and coastal scenes. This impressionist work shows his fascination for atmospheric effects and human mobility. The print was donated by Dr. Stuart and Jean Yntema in 1962 and is displayed in the upstairs porch room. (Courtesy of the Saginaw Club.)

Dr. Stuart and Jean Yntema donated this lithograph painting to the club in 1962. The original oil-on-canvas work by Thomas Hart Benton (1889–1975), titled *Louisiana Rice Fields*, is in the Brooklyn Museum. Benton was an American painter and muralist. The sculpted figures in his paintings show everyday people in scenes of life in the United States. (Courtesy of the Saginaw Club.)

Woodsmere, an oil-on-canvas painting by Katherine Hamilton Wagenhals (1883–1966), hangs in the small lounge on the second floor of the club. Wagenhals began her art studies at Smith College. She was active in Fort Wayne, Indiana, before settling in San Diego in the early 1920s. She died in San Francisco in 1966. This painting was donated by Robert S. Montague. (Courtesy of the Saginaw Club.)

The lithograph *Field of Flowers* graces the wall in the second-floor meeting room. The artist of the watercolor is Gustav Klimt, who painted a variety of subjects. Klimt was born in Vienna in 1862 and lived in relative poverty as a child. He had to support his family financially throughout his life. In 1876, Klimt was awarded a scholarship to the Vienna School of Arts and Crafts, where he studied until 1883. (Courtesy of the Saginaw Club.)

This oil painting of Shoppenagon was donated to the East Saginaw Club by Charles Willis Ward of Detroit and Eanger Irving Couse, the artist. The club accepted the painting in 1911 and made note to the donors that the artwork was appropriate because of the fact that Shoppenagon was personally known to many members and had been invited to events there. (Courtesy of the Saginaw Club.)

Artist Eanger Irving Couse is pictured with his favorite model, Ben Lujan. When Couse first traveled to New Mexico, the Santa Fe Railroad granted free trips in exchange for paintings, which were reproduced on the railroad's timetables and menus. Couse had a studio in Taos, New Mexico, where Indian models posed in a scene he constructed. Ben Lujan was used more than others. Lujan eventually took Couse's name as his own. (Authors' collection.)

This lithograph by Hoffman is untitled; it shows boatmen on a river in a forest. The work hangs on the wall in the third-floor ballroom of the Saginaw Club. It was a gift from William A. and Elizabeth Pressprich in 1993. The ballroom is used for many large group functions. (Courtesy of the Saginaw Club.)

This untitled lithograph by Hoffman painted in 1940 hangs in the third-floor ballroom of the Saginaw Club. It is a colorful picture of an Indian fishing at a waterfall. The work was donated to the club by William and Elizabeth Pressprich in 1993. William Pressprich received an award and was named an outstanding young man from the Michigan Junior Chamber of Commerce in 1962. (Courtesy of the Saginaw Club.)

This lithograph hangs on the wall of the first-floor bar room. It is a scene of early Saginaw showing Genesee Avenue from the Genesee Street Bridge. The main mode of transportation in the early 1900s was the trolley. Based on the flags flying across the street, it may have been a day of celebration in the city. (Courtesy of the Saginaw Club.)

The second lithograph in the bar room of the Saginaw Club is a scene of the early east side fire station. The fire wagons and the water pumper were drawn by horses. The firehouse was used for many years and went from horse- to gas-powered trucks. (Courtesy of the Saginaw Club.)

# *Three*

# The Saginaw Club

The East Saginaw Club was built in 1889 after a group of Saginaw businessmen planned a structure that would be a place where men could relax after a day's work. They planned a building that would house beautiful furnishings and be adorned with lovely artwork. For their enjoyment, they bought billiard tables and installed bowling alleys in the basement. They hosted parties and dinners and invited notable guests who were in town. The club went from stockholders to membership, and the name was changed to the Saginaw Club. Famous Americans, including US presidents William Howard Taft and Gerald Ford, have been entertained at the Saginaw Club.

This photograph of the building was taken after the addition over the driveway was completed. The addition is the second-floor women's powder room. The building is on Washington Avenue next to the Shrine Club. Some sources indicate that there is a time capsule located under the porch. (Courtesy of the Saginaw Club.)

Most Michigan markers are free standing, but the marker of the Saginaw Club is attached to the front of the building next to the entrance doors. The marker tells some of the history of the Saginaw Club, which has graced the main street of town for over 100 years. (Courtesy of the Saginaw Club.)

The club's entrance doors are used only on special occasions. This entryway has a leaded-glass transom and beautiful wooded doors with glass inserts with the club emblem on each. Wood was used throughout the clubhouse as most of the members were lumbermen or in the lumber industry. There are separate entrances for visitors and members. (Authors' collection.)

Entering the building from the front porch leads to the first-floor game room and lounge. Displayed over the hallway door is the motto of the Saginaw Club—which has been there since the club's opening in 1889. (Authors' collection.)

According to the minutes of the East Saginaw Club on March 5, 1890, a proposal was presented by Robert M. Randall that the furnishing committee be authorized to contract with the Garden City Company for four billiard tables in accordance with their proposal. Seven members of the board of managers voted yes. Today, the club has one billiard table located on the first floor. (Courtesy of the Saginaw Club.)

Devotees of the game of bowling had three alleys, each 62 feet long by 40 inches wide, in the basement of the clubhouse. The cost to bowl was 7½¢, because a member complained about the 10¢ charge. On February 7, 1899, a tournament was held at the club with the Greater New York Bowlers. A large attendance, including ladies, came and stayed for the lunch when the games finished. The New York team won all five games. (Authors' collection.)

The members' reading room on the first floor, which opens from the elevator, features a table laden with periodicals. Here, members could read the latest newspapers and magazines. The room holds comfortable overstuffed chairs. It is a place to relax with friends before dinner. (Courtesy of the Saginaw Club.)

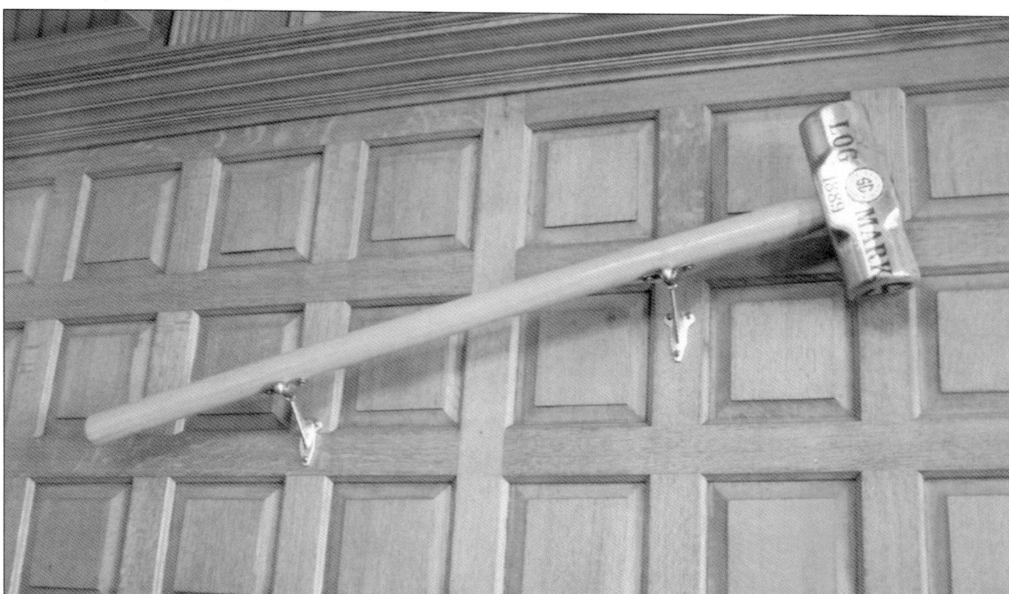


Many of the founding members of the Saginaw Club were involved in the lumbering business. Many of these men were owners of timberland. The logs from their land had to be identified before they were sent to the sawmill, so a mark was affixed to the ends of logs. A commemorative log mark with an SC on the end was presented to the club and has a prominent place over the game room fireplace. (Courtesy of the Saginaw Club.)

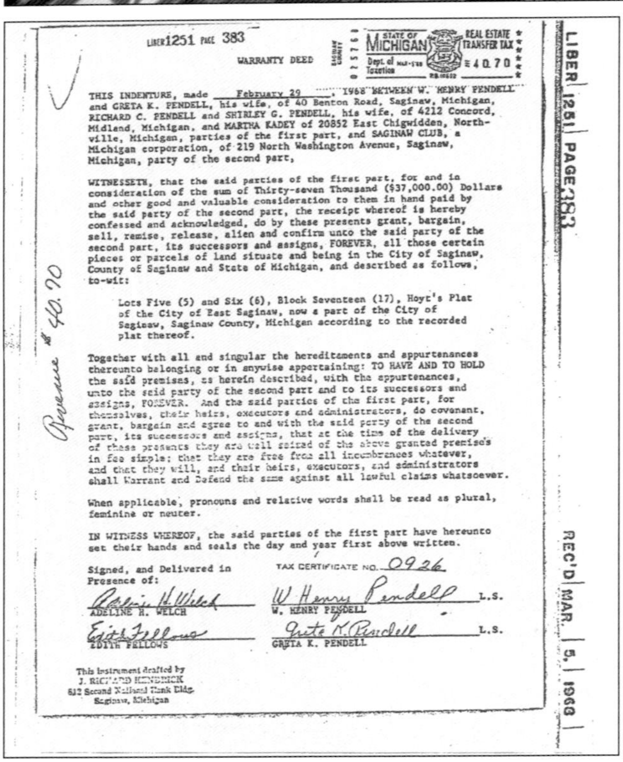

LIBER 1251 PAGE 383

WARRANTY DEED

STATE OF MICHIGAN REAL ESTATE TRANSFER TAX Dept. of Taxation $40.70

THIS INDENTURE, made February 29, 1968 BETWEEN W. HENRY PENDELL and GRETA K. PENDELL, his wife, of 40 Benton Road, Saginaw, Michigan, RICHARD C. PENDELL and SHIRLEY G. PENDELL, his wife, of 4212 Concord, Midland, Michigan, and MARTHA KADEY of 20852 East Chigwidden, Northville, Michigan, parties of the first part, and SAGINAW CLUB, a Michigan corporation, of 219 North Washington Avenue, Saginaw, Michigan, party of the second part,

WITNESSETH, that the said parties of the first part, for and in consideration of the sum of Thirty-seven Thousand ($37,000.00) Dollars and other good and valuable consideration to them in hand paid by the said party of the second part, the receipt whereof is hereby confessed and acknowledged, do by these presents grant, bargain, sell, remise, release, alien and confirm unto the said party of the second part, its successors and assigns, FOREVER, all those certain pieces or parcels of land situate and being in the City of Saginaw, County of Saginaw and State of Michigan, and described as follows, to-wit:

Lots Five (5) and Six (6), Block Seventeen (17), Hoyt's Plat of the City of East Saginaw, now a part of the City of Saginaw, Saginaw County, Michigan according to the recorded plat thereof.

Together with all and singular the hereditaments and appurtenances thereunto belonging or in anywise appertaining: TO HAVE AND TO HOLD the said premises, as herein described, with the appurtenances, unto the said party of the second part and to its successors and assigns, FOREVER. And the said parties of the first part, for themselves, their heirs, executors and administrators, do covenant, grant, bargain and agree to and with the said party of the second part, its successors and assigns, that at the time of the delivery of these presents they are well seized of the above granted premises in fee simple; that they are free from all incumbrances whatever, and that they will, and their heirs, executors, and administrators shall Warrant and Defend the same against all lawful claims whatsoever.

When applicable, pronouns and relative words shall be read as plural, feminine or neuter.

IN WITNESS WHEREOF, the said parties of the first part have hereunto set their hands and seals the day and year first above written.

Signed, and Delivered in Presence of:

TAX CERTIFICATE NO. 0926

Adeline H. Welch — ADELINE H. WELCH

W Henry Pendell L.S. — W. HENRY PENDELL

Edith Fellows — EDITH FELLOWS

Greta K. Pendell L.S. — GRETA K. PENDELL

This instrument drafted by J. RICHARD HENDRICK 612 Second National Bank Bldg. Saginaw, Michigan

Revenue # 40.70

REC'D MAR. 5, 1968

As the club grew, additional property became necessary. The first addition came in 1891 when a 35 by 60 foot lot at the rear of the club was purchased for $600. In 1965, Frank Andersen sold lots Nos. 7 and 8 of Hoyt's Plat to the club for $1. (Courtesy of the Saginaw Club.)

On February 29, 1968, Henry and Greta Pendell of Saginaw, Richard and Shirley Pendell of Midland, and Martha Kadey of Northville, Michigan, sold lots Nos. 5 and 6 of Hoyt's Plat of the city of East Saginaw, now part of the city of Saginaw, for the sum of $37,000 to the Saginaw Club. (Courtesy of Register of Deeds.)

The beautiful grandfather clock on the first floor of the Saginaw Club displays a plaque with the inscription, "Donated in memory of J. Will Grant." The plaque does not indicate the donor. J. Will Grant was a jeweler in East Saginaw and an early member of the East Saginaw Club. (Authors' collection.)

J. Will Grant was born in New York and came to Saginaw in 1871 at age 15. He began learning the jewelry business in a store at the corner of Washington and Genesee Avenues. He purchased an interest in the store and learned all aspects of the jewelry business. He became sole owner of the jewelry store and also bought an interest in the Mason Building. He was one of the promoters of the East Saginaw Club. He helped secure charter members and was instrumental in the building of the clubhouse. (Courtesy of Mills History.)

Another feature of the club reminiscent of Saginaw's lumbering days is the beautiful woodwork throughout the building. Whether it be doors, stairways, or hallways, it reminds visitors of the choices of the lumber barons to build and furnish an elegant showplace in the city. (Courtesy of the Saginaw Club.)

A small room on the second floor is used as a lounge, or on days of busy banquets at Thanksgiving, Easter, or other events, as an overflow room for diners. This small room is not used as much as other club rooms. It has at least four beautiful oil paintings on its walls. (Courtesy of the Saginaw Club.)

Located on the third floor, the ballroom echoes with the sounds of grand events of the past. It is spacious enough for large gatherings or smaller events, with an area for a dance floor. The ballroom has a bar, band stage, conversation alcove, bridal lounge, and restrooms. (Courtesy of the Saginaw Club.)

The third-floor ballroom makes every occasion special. It features soaring ceilings with flowing drapery and polished wood floors. When a speaker is engaged, the room can be filled to overflowing. There have been wedding receptions of up to 200 people. In the 1950s, there were tea dances held for families on Saturday afternoons. (Courtesy of the Saginaw Club.)

In 1903, the board of managers gave their recommendations to the stockholders for submitting bids for improvements and an addition to the clubhouse. W.T. Cooper was chosen as the architect. The cost of the new addition, which would include a porch in the rear, was $6,500. This did not include furnishings, but $10,000 covered the entire expense. (Courtesy of the Saginaw Club.)

On Saturday, March 3, 2019, the Saginaw Club had a celebration to mark the retirement of the club's mortgage. This was a member appreciation event, which featured cuisine of the French Riviera. Also, there was a Monte Carlo–themed casino night. The club now has a cash flow to make many capital improvements that have been needed for some time. (Courtesy of the Saginaw Club.)

# *Four*

# EVENTS

There are always interesting happenings at the Saginaw Club. Beginning with the yearly toast to the office of the president in January, each month has something interesting planned. There have been events in the past that members remembered and enjoyed. Some of these were the Club Grub, which included three other area clubs. There have been excursions to plays and sporting events. At the club, there are always the traditional events, such as the Razzies and stag nights.

Each January 1, one club member gives the toast to the office of the president of the United States. The presenter is unknown until he is introduced at the event. The toast is held in the third-floor ballroom and each person in attendance is given a glass of champagne to toast the president at the conclusion of the talk. Thomas Basil is pictured giving the toast. (Courtesy of the Saginaw Club.)

The Razzies is a group of longer tenured members who meet monthly for breakfast or lunch. Razzies participants shown here are, from left to right, unidentified, Hiel Rockwell Jr., General David Hall, and Louis Furlo. (Courtesy of the Saginaw Club.)

In 1991 and 1992, the Club Grub was held between four local clubs. Each club featured a different theme at its location. Entertainment at the Germania Town and Country Club featured accordion players from Frankenmuth. A variety of German sausages and other German dishes were there to be sampled by participants. (Courtesy of the Saginaw Club.)

For two years, the Saginaw Club joined with the Bay City Country Club, the Saginaw Country Club, and the Germania Town and Country Club for the Club Grub. Traveling between clubs by bus, the members enjoyed different cuisines at each destination. This mariachi group entertained at the Saginaw Country Club, where Mexican food was on the menu. (Courtesy of the Saginaw Club.)

For several years, the Saginaw Club has celebrated the birthday of Robert Burns, Scotland's favorite son. He is widely known as the national poet of Scotland. He was born January 25, 1759, and died July 21, 1796, at age 37. Tributes to his life and work are held worldwide at Burns Suppers. In 2019, the Saginaw Club celebrated the dinner on January 25, Burns's 260th birthday. (Courtesy of the Saginaw Club.)

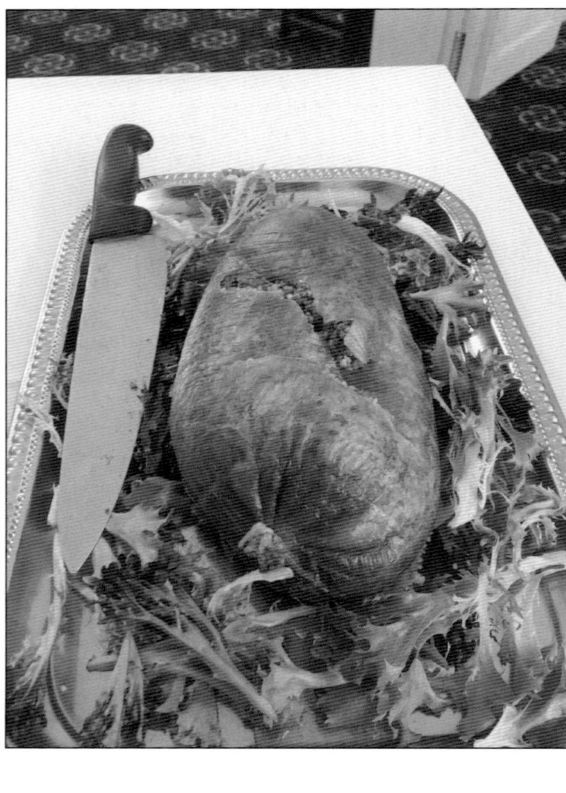

No Burns Supper would be complete without haggis, drink (normally whisky), songs, recitals, and fun. To make Haggis, a sheep's stomach is cleaned and soaked in cold salted water. For the filling, the lungs, heart, and liver are boiled about two hours. When cooked, the meat is minced and mixed with onion, oatmeal, salt, pepper, coriander, mace, and nutmeg. The mixture is spooned into the sheep's stomach, sewn up with strong thread, and placed in boiling water to cook for three hours. It is then cut open and served with mashed turnips and mashed potatoes. (Courtesy of the Saginaw Club.)

The Burns Supper on January 25, 2019, was hosted by George and Janie Gugino and Greg and Ann Branch. These kilt wearers who participated in the celebration are, from left to right, Peter Sulfridge, Robert Emerick, Greg Branch, Dr. George Gugino, and George Stewart. After the meal, there was a toast to the memory of Robert Burns. The evening ended with a chorus of Auld Lang Syne. (Authors' collection.)

A bagpiper pipes the guests into the dining room, then "The Selkirk Grace" by Robert Burns is read. Next is the piping in of the haggis, followed by the toast to the haggis and the chairman's welcome. Here, Dr. George Gugino delivers the Selkirk Grace: "Some have meat and canna eat, and some wad eat that want it. But we have meat and we can eat, and sae the Lord be thankit." (Courtesy of the Saginaw Club.)

The Saginaw Club celebrated its 100th anniversary in 1989. Many activities were planned, including a members' dinner. A wooden plaque was designed with a picture of the original clubhouse. Miniature plaques with the same design were available for members. At the dinner, a plate from Syracuse China with the picture of the clubhouse in the center was also available to members. (Courtesy of the Saginaw Club.)

An anniversary three-tiered cake was served as dessert after dinner. A scrapbook with articles saved from newspapers was displayed. The articles were of important events in the life of the club. (Courtesy of the Saginaw Club.)

Thomas and Ruth McDonald arrive at the Saginaw Club for the 100th anniversary celebration. The couple arrived in one of Tom's cars from his classic car collection. Tom McDonald was the president of the club in 1989. (Courtesy of the Saginaw Club.)

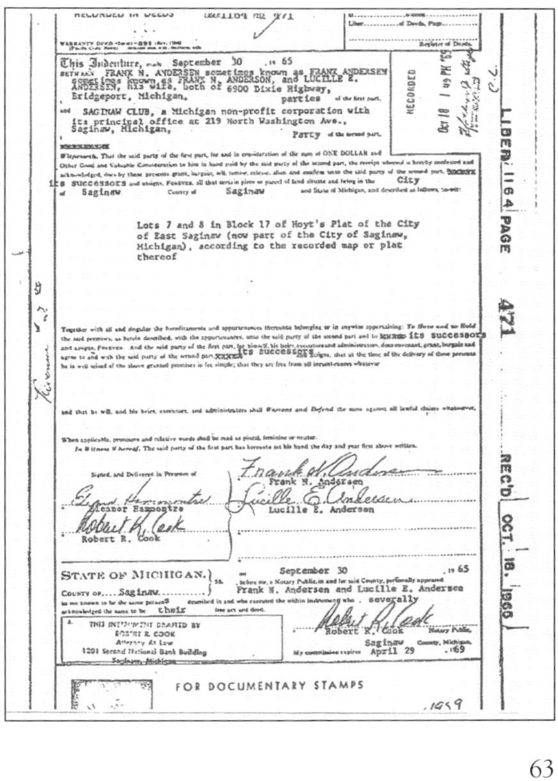

RECORDED IN DEEDS LIBER 1164 PAGE 471

WARRANTY DEED

This Indenture, made September 30, 19 65

BETWEEN FRANK N. ANDERSEN sometimes known as FRANK ANDERSEN sometimes known as FRANK N. ANDERSON, and LUCILLE E. ANDERSEN, his wife, both of 6900 Dixie Highway, Bridgeport, Michigan, parties of the first part,

and SAGINAW CLUB, a Michigan non-profit corporation with its principal office at 219 North Washington Ave., Saginaw, Michigan, Party of the second part,

RECORDED Oct 18 1 49 PM '65

Witnesseth, That the said party of the first part, for and in consideration of the sum of ONE DOLLAR and Other Good and Valuable Consideration to him in hand paid by the said party of the second part, the receipt whereof is hereby confessed and acknowledged, does by these presents grant, bargain, sell, remise, release, alien and confirm unto the said party of the second part, its successors and assigns, Forever, all that certain piece or parcel of land situate and being in the City of Saginaw County of Saginaw and State of Michigan, and described as follows, to-wit:

Lots 7 and 8 in Block 17 of Hoyt's Plat of the City of East Saginaw (now part of the City of Saginaw, Michigan), according to the recorded map or plat thereof

Together with all and singular the hereditaments and appurtenances thereunto belonging or in anywise appertaining: To Have and to Hold the said premises, as herein described, with the appurtenances, unto the said party of the second part and to its successors and assigns, Forever. And the said party of the first part, for himself, his heirs, executors and administrators, does covenant, grant, bargain and agree to and with the said party of the second part, its successors and assigns, that at the time of the delivery of these presents he is well seised of the above granted premises in fee simple; that they are free from all incumbrances whatever

and that he will, and his heirs, executors, and administrators shall Warrant and Defend the same against all lawful claims whatsoever.

When applicable, pronouns and relative words shall be read as plural, feminine or neuter.

In Witness Whereof, The said party of the first part has hereunto set his hand the day and year first above written.

Signed, and Delivered in Presence of

Eleanor Hamoontre

Robert R. Cook

Frank N. Andersen

Lucille E. Andersen

STATE OF MICHIGAN, COUNTY OF Saginaw } ss. — September 30, 19 65, before me, a Notary Public, in and for said County, personally appeared Frank N. Andersen and Lucille E. Andersen to me known to be the same persons described in and who executed the within instrument who severally acknowledged the same to be their free act and deed.

THIS INSTRUMENT DRAFTED BY ROBERT R. COOK Attorney At Law 1201 Second National Bank Building Saginaw, Michigan

Robert R. Cook Notary Public, Saginaw County, Michigan. My commission expires April 29, 1969

FOR DOCUMENTARY STAMPS

REC'D OCT. 18, 1965

Attending the 100th anniversary celebration were two longtime members, Frank N. Andersen and Albert L. Riedel. Riedel was president of Michigan Bean. Frank Andersen was passionate about giving to his community and making life better for his fellow citizens. He remains one of the region's best-known philanthropists. Pictured is the deed in which Andersen sold lots to the Saginaw Club for $1. (Courtesy of the Register of Deeds.)

Club members enjoy a black-tie event celebrating the Saginaw Club's 100th anniversary. From left to right are (first row) club manager David Wagner, Thomas McDonald Sr., Peter Nagel, Terry Niederstadt, Paul Virciglio, B.J. Humphreys, and Thomas Weadock; (second row) Joseph Day, Donald Jueneman, Robert Kendrick, and Thomas Cline. (Courtesy of the Saginaw Club.)

These attendees at the club's 100th anniversary celebration are, from left to right, (sitting) club manager David Wagner, unidentified, Albert S. Harvey, and Thomas McDonald Sr.; (standing) C. Ward Lauderbach, Herbert W. McLachlan, Daniel W. Toshach, Alvin G. Benson, Robert G. App, Gilbert A. Deibel, John C. Bintz, and club manager Chester Pochopien. (Courtesy of the Saginaw Club.)

A tradition begun years ago is the Five o'clock Club. That is the time most of the members were available to relax after work at the Saginaw Club. Usually meeting at the clubhouse, any member was welcome. In June 1988, the Five o'clock Club met at the estate of Thomas McDonald. (Courtesy of the Saginaw Club.)

Stag nights are held at the Saginaw Club on a monthly basis. As early as the 1930s, widows of members were allowed to join. Other women were admitted starting in 1980. Now that women are members and two have been elected president, stag nights are not exclusively male. Pictured here enjoying fellowship of other members are, from left to right, James Krohn, Dr. Samuel Shaheen, Richard Katz, unidentified, and Louis Furlo. (Courtesy of the Saginaw Club.)

In 1989, the club's 100th year, a tree was planted as a celebration. Pictured are Thomas McDonald, club president; Dr. William Scharffe, membership chairman; and Dr. William Bow, assistant chairman. (Courtesy of the Saginaw Club.)

A group of members gather on the lawn and porch in celebration of the club's 100th anniversary and the successful membership drive. The choice was to plant a white pine, the state tree, but it was determined that they do not thrive if exposed to exhaust fumes. A red pine was planted instead. (Courtesy of the Saginaw Club.)

Stag night on November 10, 2010, hosted the club's first ever salute to the club's past presidents. Nearly 40 members attended the event. Pictured are, from left to right, (sitting) Dr. William Scharffe, Robert Kendrick, Heidi Bolger, John Kunitzer, and John Bintz; (standing) David Turner, John Princing, Brian Eggers, James Tiderington, Gary Glaza, Carrington Beach Day, and Robert Sidney. (Courtesy of the Saginaw Club.)

This poster, "Our Michigan Friends," depicts original Saginaw Club members shown in caricature form. The drawings are from a 1904 lithographed book of iconic Michigan individuals from other cities. The men are shown in their fields of endeavor. The poster is on the wall in the grill room. (Courtesy of the Saginaw Club.)

When Jack Provenzano was club president, he had the idea to invite family and friends to an event during the holidays. Provenzano hosted a casual reception for members and their family and friends who are in town for the holidays. The chef prepared some delicious heavy hors d'oeuvres, and attendees enjoyed renewing old acquaintances. The tickets included two drink tokens. (Courtesy of the Saginaw Club.)

Club members, their families, and friends who are in town celebrating the holidays in Saginaw are invited to the annual event. The first gathering was held in 2016 and has become a tradition, welcoming home people who have the opportunity to celebrate with family and friends during the festive time of year. In 2018, the John Morey family attended the event. Shown here are, from left to right, John, Lara Morey, Cindy Morey, Cassidy Morey, and the girls' fiancés, Matt Morgrette and Andrew Price. (Courtesy of Saginaw Club.)

# *Five*

# Members

The charter members of the East Saginaw Club bought stock for $100 when the club was organized. In 1919, the original articles of association changed from stock ownership to membership. In the years since the club's inception, the number of members has changed. There was a time when the number of members was limited to 250. The number has changed and now is over 300.

Richard J. Garber, Saginaw Club member, is a lifelong Saginaw resident. He is the third-generation owner of Garber Buick in Saginaw. He graduated from Douglas MacArthur High School and has an associate's degree and a bachelor of science degree from Northwood University. Garber has made service to the community a major priority in his life. He has received numerous awards, among them the Frank N. Andersen Spirit of Philanthropy Award presented by the Saginaw Community Foundation. In 2002, he became owner and governor of an Ontario Hockey League franchise, now the Saginaw Spirit. (Courtesy of the Garber Automotive Group.)

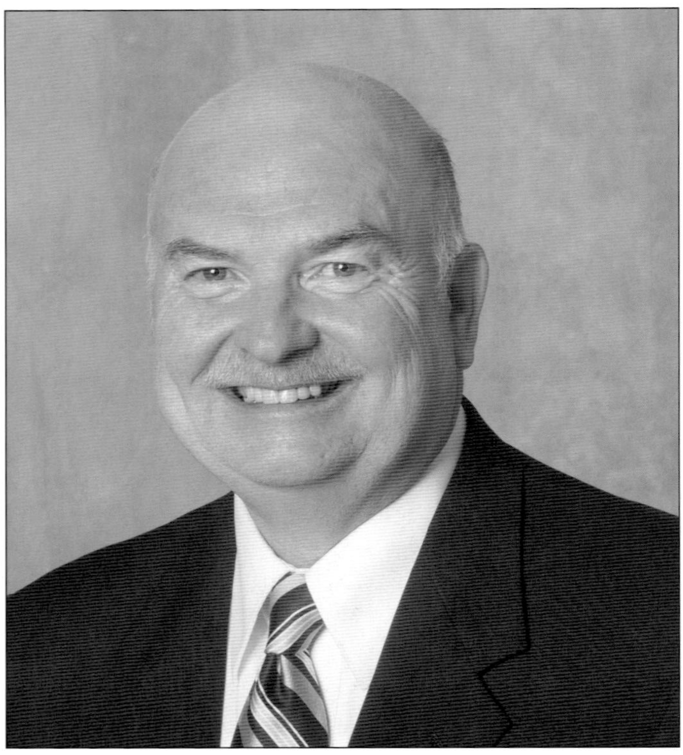

Gary Fahndrich has been the owner of West Side Decorating since purchasing the business from his father in 1982. He has always been active in the Saginaw community. Since the early 1970s, he has been a member of local service organizations. He is a member of the Rotary Club of Saginaw and the Fordney Club. He has served on the board of directors of the Saginaw County Chamber of Commerce. Fahndrich enjoys volunteering for Habitat for Humanity and is a proud member of the Saginaw Club. (Courtesy of Gary Fahndrich.)

Frank A. Picard, born in Saginaw, received a bachelor of laws degree from the University of Michigan in 1912. In 1913, he was an assistant prosecuting attorney, and from 1913 to 1917 he was in private practice. He was a captain in the US Army from 1917 to 1919. When he returned to Saginaw he served as city attorney, and was a candidate for the US Senate in 1934. Picard was nominated by Pres. Franklin D. Roosevelt to the US District Court for Eastern Michigan in 1939. (Courtesy of the Picard family.)

Frank Picard came from a Saginaw family of 10 children. Several of his older brothers, billed as the "Flying Picards," performed as aerialists with major circuses around the country. Frank excelled at anything he attempted. At Saginaw High School, he was quarterback and captain of the football team and made a name for himself playing football at the University of Michigan, where he was also an outstanding law student. (Courtesy of the Picard family.)

Tony D'Anna grew up in the Down River Detroit area. He spent his early career in the automotive industry. He later moved to Chattanooga, Tennessee, with the Rockwell International Corporation as a plant manager. D'Anna always wanted to be self-employed, and decided to pursue a franchise business. He was offered a McDonald's restaurant in Frankenmuth, Michigan, in 1983. Since then, he and his wife, Geraldine, have continued to build and grow their business and have become a major part of all the communities that they serve. (Courtesy of Tony D'Anna.)

In 1957, Dick Katz left Abbott Plumbing & Heating to form a partnership with Robert Remer. The two started Remer Plumbing & Heating, with Remer in charge of residential and Katz in charge of the commercial division. Upon Remer's retirement in 1990, Katz became president of the company. In 1991, he was named contractor of the year by the Michigan Plumbing and Mechanical Contractors Association. Pictured are, from left to right, Dick Katz, Bishop Cistone, and Mark Katz. (Authors' collection.)

Guy Garber, a life member of the Saginaw Club, and his son Richard Garber Sr. are enjoying fly fishing on the Au Sable River. Many members of the club were avid outdoorsmen. While they enjoyed fishing and hunting, they were also concerned with conservation of the state's resources. The grayling was native to the river, but slowly vanished because of unregulated fishing pressure, and trout were introduced. (Courtesy of the Garber family.)

Guy and Richard Garber fished for trout on the North Branch of the Au Sable River. The Au Sable rises northwest of Grayling, the city named for the native fish. During the lumber era, the Au Sable River floated timber to the mills. Two dams helped move the lumber downstream. The dams have been removed, and the grayling population dwindled. In 1889, brown trout were introduced. Later, brook and rainbow trout were added. (Authors' collection.)

These three future Saginaw Club members, pictured in their football years at St. Andrew's High School, are, from left to right, Emil Tessin, who became a well-known architect of prefab homes and buildings; Jack Rehmann, who began an accounting firm in 1941, which became Rehmann, Robson & Company; and Hugo Baumann, who was a World War II hero. (Authors' collection.)

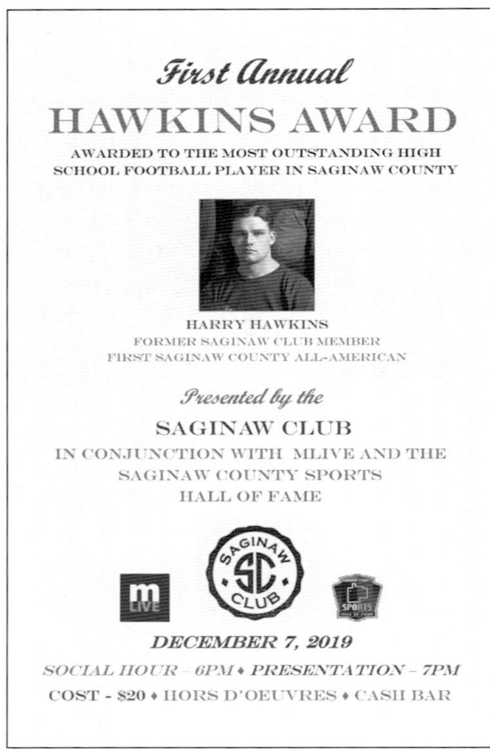


Pictured is a program honoring Harry Hawkins. Hawkins won honors in scholastics, sports, industry, and civic endeavors. He won Arthur Hill High School's Ippel Cup in 1922 and was its honored alumnus in 1961. He was an All-American tackle at the University of Michigan and a 1926 graduate of the School of Engineering. He was employed by General Motors and was a director at Saginaw Steering Gear. (Courtesy of the Saginaw Club.)

Fred L. Borchard is one of three members of the Borchard family who have served the citizens of Saginaw and the State of Michigan as judges. Fred's father, former chief judge Fred J. Borchard, has been recognized as the longest-sitting judge in the history of the state, serving 53 years. Judge Fred L. Borchard has served 20 years, and his younger brother James T. Borchard is in his ninth year of service. Fred L. Borchard is recognized as Saginaw's first chief judge of all Saginaw courts, district, probate, and circuit. Judge Fred L. Borchard has served as president of the Michigan judges' association for trial court and appellate judges. He has also served as chairman of the judicial counsel, made up of representatives from the three courts. In addition, he has served on the chief justice's counsel for the Michigan Supreme Court and as a delegate to the National Center for State Trial Courts. He currently is a board member for the Michigan Supreme Court Historical Society. Judge Borchard was instrumental in initiating specialty courts, which included the Swift and Sure Program. (Courtesy of Judge Borchard.)

The Morley Brothers business began during the heyday of the lumber era in Michigan and experienced ups and downs for 100 years. Control of the company transitioned to Louis J. Furlo Sr., who was elected president in 1978, with Burrows Morley remaining as chairman of the board. A Morley Brothers employee, Furlo began working there in 1959 as a sales associate. As part of a restructuring plan, Furlo sold Morley Brothers to S&T Industries of Louisville, Kentucky, the nation's then-largest wholesale hardware company. In 1982, Furlo and a group of investors purchased the Incentive Division from S&T Industries. Morley Incentives has expanded into additional services that complemented incentive travel. Today, Morley is owned and operated by Furlo's three sons, Paul W. Furlo, Christopher J. Furlo, and Louis J. Furlo Jr. The company has continued to grow, adding new jobs and winning employment awards. Between 2008 and 2011, Morley experienced rapid expansion and more than doubled in size. Morley ranks number four in the top-40 primary employers in Saginaw. Seen below are, from left to right, Christopher, Louis Sr., Paul, and Louis Furlo Jr.. (Courtesy of the Saginaw Club.)

David D. Hoffman has been a judge in the 70th District Court in Saginaw since January 2017. He was in private practice for 29 years before becoming a judge. Judge Hoffman is a graduate of St. Stephen High School, Michigan State University (1985), and DePaul University College of Law (1988). He has served the community on a number of boards and commissions throughout Saginaw County and has been a member of the Saginaw Club for over 20 years. (Courtesy of Hon. Judge Hoffman.)

Judge Hoffman officiated at the wedding of Cassidy Morey and Andrew Price in September 2018 at the picturesque Montague Inn in Saginaw. The inn was built in 1929 by Robert Montague. The property is located on Washington Avenue and borders Lake Linton (a slip of the Saginaw River) to the west. It is a popular destination for weddings, anniversaries, and other group events. Pictured in the library are the judge and the bride and groom. (Authors' collection.)

Max P. Heavenrich Sr. is listed as a member of the East Saginaw Club in the 1907–1908 club booklet. He attended Saginaw Schools and went on to receive a civil engineering degree from the University of Michigan. He worked in this profession for three years before returning to Saginaw, where he entered the mercantile business that his family had established. He also headed the Heavenrich Realty Company, which owned a number of properties in downtown Saginaw. (Courtesy of the Castle Museum.)

Brothers Sam, Max, and Carl Heavenrich established the mercantile business Heavenrich Brothers and Company in 1882. Max's son Max P. left his engineering profession to join the Saginaw business. All three of the brothers were members of the East Saginaw Club and were respected businessmen in East Saginaw. They also had an interest in education. The firm established the first Saginaw scholarship in 1891. Max P. was a civic leader, and in recognition of his work, an east side school was named in his honor. (Courtesy of the Castle Museum.)

The Garber Buick dealership was originally located at 208 North Washington Avenue across from the Temple Theatre. The company sold Buick and Pontiac automobiles. In the 1948 Saginaw directory, the automobiles were advertised "with all the basic prewar quality, plus impressive improvements." Complete service and accessory sales were also available at the dealership. (Courtesy of the Garber Company.)

Richard Garber Sr., sales manager of Garber Buick (left), and Brady Denton, salesman, are celebrating the fact that Denton was the one-millionth stockholder of AT&T stock. He bought seven shares of stock from a customer who sold it to Denton so he could buy a new Buick. (Courtesy of the Garber Company.)

Frank N. Andersen (left) and Albert Riedel (right) were longtime members of the Saginaw Club. Andersen was born in New York in 1889 and moved to Saginaw in 1923. Lacking a college education, he acquired his knowledge of engineering through experience and correspondence courses. He started his own business in 1929. First was Andersen's Sand and Gravel Company, followed in 1936 by Ready Mix Concrete and in 1954 by Andersen Builders' Supply Company. Throughout the years, Andersen made major contributions to the community. In 1962, he was honored at Delta College by receiving the President's Medal, which is the highest award the institution offers. Albert Riedel was born in 1892 in Minden, Michigan. With an eighth-grade certificate, he qualified to enter Michigan State Agricultural College. He was president and general manager of the Michigan Bean Company. He made the Jack Rabbit brand of beans known all over the world. While he was president, the famous jumping bean bunny neon sign was erected on the world's largest bean elevator. (Courtesy of the Saginaw Club.)

"One Mile in One Day" is engraved on a brass plate sent by Pres. Dwight D. Eisenhower honoring F. Roland Sargent and the Sargent Construction Company's achievement. The greatest public works project in history was in full swing (1956–1966) with the passage of the Federal Aid Highway Act of 1956. During the European theater campaign in Germany, Sargent became a judge advocate on General Eisenhower's staff. While in Germany, Eisenhower and Sargent discussed the German autobahn system of highways and foresaw the same thing happening in the United States after the war. Sargent headed back to Saginaw to enter into business with his father. The former Bridgeport Core Sand Company became Sargent Sand Company with Rolly Sargent as president. He kept in contact with Eisenhower and convinced his father to pursue the highway construction business. The Sargent Company paved Interstate Highway 75 from the Kentucky border to Sault Ste. Marie, Michigan. (Both, courtesy of the Sargent family.)

George Humphrey (1890–1970) graduated from Saginaw High School in 1908 and went on to become one of the nation's mightiest industrialists. He was a member of the East Saginaw Club, and in 1918, requested that his membership be changed from resident to nonresident status. He was chairman of the board of the M.A. Hanna Company of Cleveland. From 1953 to 1957, he was secretary of the US Treasury during the Eisenhower administration. (Authors' collection.)

Raymond L. Gover (1927–2018) was a vice president of the Saginaw Club in 1981. He became editor of the *Saginaw News* in 1970 and editor of the *Flint Journal* in 1976. In 1978, he became publisher of the *Saginaw News*. He was named its editor and publisher in 1980. He left Michigan to become publisher of the *Patriot News* in Harrisburg, Pennsylvania. (Courtesy of the Saginaw Club.)

A reception was held at the Saginaw Club for Joseph D. Frost on his 86th birthday. Frost was the former Saginaw County Republican chairman. Vice Pres. Gerald Ford and Helen Milliken, Michigan's first lady, congratulate Frost. (Courtesy of the Saginaw Club.)

Attending the birthday celebration for Joseph D. Frost at the Saginaw Club are, from left to right, club president Robert Grant, Frost, Vice President Ford, Helen Milliken, Lt. Gov. James Brickley, Congressman Al Cederberg, state Republican chairman William McLaughlin, and Gov. William Milliken. (Courtesy of Rummel Studio, Frankenmuth, Michigan.)

Andrew Ellis was born in Moundsville, West Virginia, and started selling brooms at the Moundsville State Prison when he was only 16 years old. After coming to Saginaw, he started his own beer distributing business, ending up as a very successful businessman. When he passed away at age 60, Ron Seamon succeeded him as president of the business. Ellis was a member of the Saginaw Club and a two-year president of the Saginaw Country Club. He was a board member of Saginaw General Hospital. He was an avid hunter and fisherman and loved his place on the Au Sable River. (Courtesy of the Saginaw Country Club.)

After graduating from Michigan State University, Ronald Seamon worked for the Andrew Ellis Beer Distributing Company and was involved in many civic endeavors. He was on the Saginaw General Board for six years and was president of the visiting nurses association. He was president of the Saginaw Country Club and a board member of the Saginaw Club. After moving to Hilton Head, South Carolina, he was the owner of a restaurant outfitters and president of the Shipyard Golf Club. (Courtesy of the Saginaw Country Club.)

All of the Spence brothers were members of the Saginaw Club. Edwin A. Spence was the third of the second generation to join the Spence Brothers company. He was added to the payroll in 1928 as field superintendent. With the added manpower of the other three Spences, who were all second generation, the company was able to assume more work, and this growth led to the founders' decision to incorporate in 1930. (Courtesy of the Spence Company.)

Spence Brothers, a Michigan corporation, came into being on April 1, 1930, under the management of officers and directors Hugh Spence, Matthew J. Spence, Arthur M. Spence, and Herbert A. Spence (pictured). The company has survived through times of prosperity and depression and celebrated its 100th year in business in 2010. Founding brothers Hugh and Matthew passed away in 1922 and 1948, respectively. Among the well-known buildings constructed by Spence Brothers are Crisler Arena in Ann Arbor and Eisenhower High School in Saginaw. (Courtesy of the Spence Company.)

Shaheen Development was started more than 50 years ago by Dr. Samuel Shaheen and his wife, Patricia. The couple looked after everything, from land acquisition to bookkeeping, while caring for a busy medical practice and their family. They committed to invest in their community, and Shaheen Development became one of the Great Lakes Bay Region's most successful real estate development firms. The majestic Temple Theatre in downtown Saginaw was rescued from the wrecking ball and restored to its early-20th-century splendor under the leadership of the Shaheens. They donated the completed project to the community in 2012, forming the Temple Theatre Foundation to sustain it for future generations. Dr. Shaheen passed away in 2013, and his sons Samuel and Peter now uphold the family vision, legacy, and steadfast commitment to the communities of the Great Lakes Bay Region. President and chief executive officer of Shaheen Development today is Dr. Samuel Shaheen. Peter Shaheen, vice president, leads the teams from land acquisition to construction, to ribbon-cutting, and to occupancy of the many projects. (Courtesy of Shaheen Development.)

In 2014, the Saginaw Club celebrated its 125th anniversary. It was a red-carpet affair attended by current and former members. A red carpet was laid on the walk leading to the porch stairs. The celebration was held on May 8, which was an evening of beautiful weather in Saginaw. Crowds gathered on the porch to renew old friendships. An anniversary book was published as a keepsake. (Courtesy of the Saginaw Club.)

At the 125th anniversary celebration on May 8, 2014, current and former members came together to renew old friendships. Pictured are, from left to right, unidentified, Robert Vitito, and Donald Jueneman. At the time of the celebration, Jueneman was the chief executive officer of Saginaw General Hospital. Robert Vitito was the chief executive officer of Citizens Banking Corporation and a member of the Saginaw Valley State University (SVSU) Board of Control. He was involved in many other community organizations. Vitito and his wife, Marianne, established the Vitito Global Leadership Institute at SVSU. (Authors' collection.)

The YMCA board and advisory group were in attendance at a recognition dinner on October 11, 1960, following the dedication of the new YMCA on Fordney Street. Pictured are, from left to right, (first row) Alex Levinsohn, Charles S. Crittenden, Edward B. Morley, R. Raymond Campau, Eric F. Wieneke, Herbert F. Russell, Robert H. Cook, and Guy S. Garber; (second row) Burrows Morley, Harold T. Slaght, Archie McMillan, Roswell Burrows, Elmer E. Braun, Richard J. Garber, Harry Hawkins, J. Coral Richardson, E. Colbert Ryan, Harry E. Miles, Earl W. Graft, Harvey D. Spaulding, Dr. William J. Mason, and Bryson McCulloch. (Authors' collection.)

# *Six*

# Club Presidents

Beginning with Oscar F. Wisner in 1889–1891, there have been 28 presidents of the East Saginaw Club. With the name change to the Saginaw Club in 1919, there have been 102 more people who have held the office of president of the club. Only two women have served as presidents: Heidi Bolger in 2009 and Renee Johnston in 2019. The presidents have been business leaders, educators, physicians, and community leaders. They have all taken their position seriously and kept the traditions of the Saginaw Club alive.

Brian Eggers was born and raised in Saginaw. He started AKT Peerless Environmental Services in Saginaw in 1989. The firm has now grown with offices across the nation. He was president of the Saginaw Club in 2005. Eggers is past chairman of the board of the Saginaw County Chamber of Commerce, vice president of the Michigan Chamber of Commerce, and past chairman of the St. Mary's Hospital Foundation. In Lansing, he currently serves as the governor-appointed chairman of the Michigan Underground Storage Tank Authority and the Michigan Water Use Advisory Committee. He now resides in the Bay City area with his wife, Lindsay, and their four children. (Courtesy of Brian Eggers.)

Robert H. Tiderington was born in Detroit. He first was employed by the Detroit Ball Bearing Company. After moving to Saginaw, he had the opportunity to purchase Flack-Pennell, which later merged with J. George Fischer, forming Fischer-Flack Inc., where he served as president. Tiderington was involved in community affairs. He was the president of the Saginaw Township public schools board; president of the United Way; chairman of the board of directors of St. Lukes Hospital, and a member of the operating committee of Saginaw Medical Center. He was president of the Saginaw Club in 1981, a member of the Saginaw Country Club, and a life member of Germania Town and Country Club. Among his awards were an honorary doctor of laws degree from SVSU and the Robert H. Albert Community Service Award. (Courtesy of the Saginaw News.)

Elected in 2019, Renee Johnston is the second woman to hold the office of president of the Saginaw Club. She is a native of Saginaw and a graduate of Michigan Lutheran Seminary, Alma College, and Valparaiso University School of Law. After graduating from law school, she began a nine-year career with Delphi Corporation in Saginaw. She transferred to a Delphi division in Troy, Michigan, as a human resources manager. Next, she had an opportunity to change careers that brought her back to Saginaw. She accepted the position of president and chief executive officer of the Saginaw Community Foundation, a nonprofit organization whose mission is to fulfill donors' wishes and enable community initiatives to come to life. Because of her community involvement, she has been recognized with many awards. As a member of the Junior League of Saginaw, she was awarded the Junior League Gold Rose. In 2008, Johnston was named the Outstanding Fundraising Executive of the Year. She was appointed by Gov. Rick Snyder to the Michigan Board of Medicine, among other honors. (Courtesy of Renee Johnston.)

Gary Glaza, president of the Saginaw Club in 2002, is chief financial officer of Shaheen Development. He has been in this position for over 12 years following a 36-year career with Second National Bank/Citizens Bank, where he was the regional president for the northern half of the state of Michigan. Glaza holds a bachelor of business administration from Northwood University and is a graduate of the Graduate School of Banking, University of Wisconsin, Madison. He is currently the chairman of the Temple Theatre Foundation, the secretary/treasurer of the Saginaw Art Museum, vice chairman of the Saginaw County Land Bank Authority, vice chairman of the Downtown Development Authority of the City of Saginaw, and former board member of the St. Mary's of Michigan Foundation. He has also been involved in many community organizations. (Courtesy of Gary Glaza.)

David Abbs specializes in investment management, retirement planning, and employee benefits for his clients, including professionals, pre-retirees, retirees, and small businesses. He has been working with clients in the Great Lakes Bay Region since 1981. He is involved in many community organizations, including the Saginaw Community Foundation, the Saginaw Valley Rotary, the Saginaw Art Museum, and the Saginaw County Chamber of Commerce, among others. He has been a member of the Saginaw Club since 1992 and served as president in 2011. (Courtesy of David Abbs.)

Guy S. Garber was one of the nation's leading auto dealers. In his early years, he met and was hired by Will C. Durant, the founder of General Motors. In 1912, he became the Buick distributor in Saginaw. Until 1965, he held the only dealer-distributor contract with the Buick division of General Motors. He was a leader in community fundraising events. He founded the Saginaw Society for Crippled Children, helped guide the Saginaw YMCA, served on the West Side Board of Education, and helped consolidate the East and West Side School Districts. He was president of the Saginaw Club in 1931. (Courtesy of the Saginaw Club.)

Club members Guy Garber (right) and his father in law, John M. Denyes, are discussing the size of the fish they caught. The men enjoyed fly fishing on the Au Sable River. Guy Garber was concerned with conservation of the state's resources. The native fish to the Au Sable was the grayling, which slowly vanished because of unregulated fishing pressure; later, different types of trout were introduced. (Courtesy of the Garber Company.)

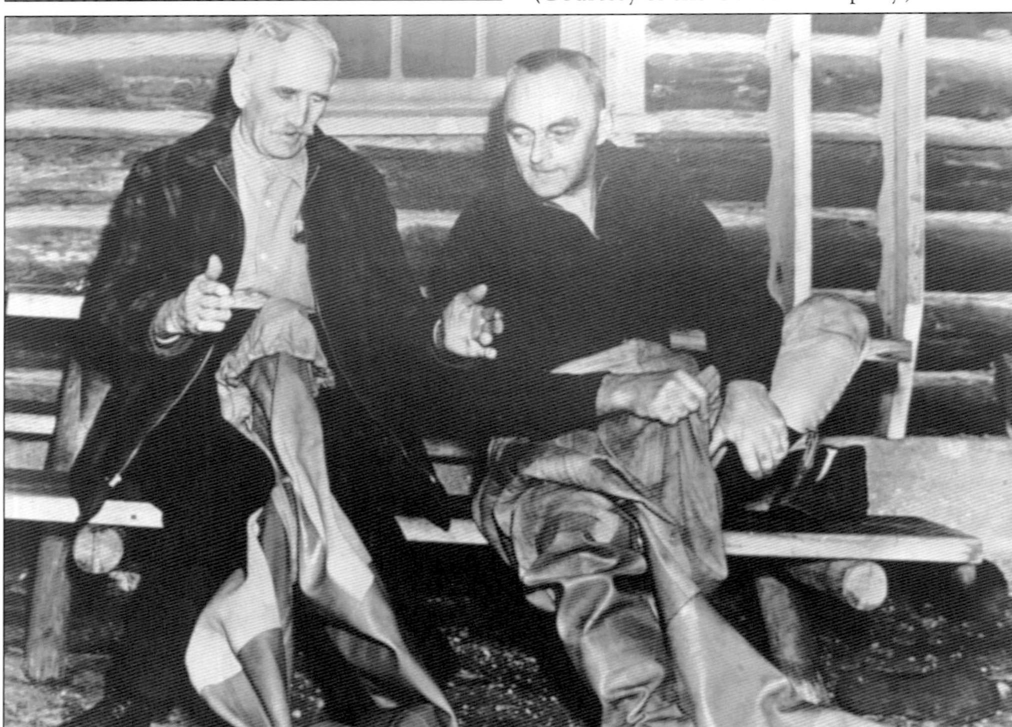

These former club presidents gathered for a group portrait in 2013. From left to right are (first row) John Kunitzer, David Schooltz, Thomas McDonald, and John Bintz; (second row) Gary Glaza, Timothy Royle, John Princing, Michael Day, Thomas McDonald Jr., David Turner, Dr. William Scharffe, David Abbs, Kenneth MacDonald Jr., Brian Eggers, and Heidi Bolger. (Courtesy of the Saginaw Club.)

Mark Hardy, club president in 2018, has been a wealth management advisor with Northwestern Mutual for 28 years. He is an insurance agent of Northwestern Mutual and Northwestern Long Term Care Insurance Company in Milwaukee, Wisconsin. He and his wife, Kathy, have three daughters and two grandchildren. They live in Bay City and enjoy being members of the Saginaw Club, the Saginaw Country Club, and the Huntsman Hunt Club in Dryden. Mark enjoys golfing, shooting sporting clays, and fly fishing, and is a high school varsity basketball official. (Courtesy of Mark Hardy.)

Heidi Bolger is a founding principal of the consulting division of Rehmann, Robson & Company. She consults with businesses in the areas of mergers and acquisitions, strategy, succession planning, profit improvement, and valuation. She has been with the company for 35 years and has served as an advisor to a multitude of businesses and organizations. In 2009, she had the distinction of being elected the first woman president of the Saginaw Club. (Courtesy of Heidi Bolger.)

Heidi Bolger and her family own the Iron Fish Distillery. This business is Michigan's first working farm solely dedicated to distilling small-batch craft spirits. The family reclaimed a late 1890s abandoned farmstead with the mission to create exceptional spirits from the ground up. Using practices that respect the health of nearby watersheds, the Bolgers grow their own grain, as well as source grain from Michigan farmers. The business cares about its employees, its community, and the land. (Courtesy of Heidi Bolger.)

Robert B. Frantz was one of Saginaw's best-known architects. In 1920, he worked for the firm of Cowles and Muttschler. He soon set up his own office in the Chase Building on 116 North Washington Avenue. His first big job was the American State Bank, later Michigan National, on the corner of Lapeer Avenue and Genesee Street. In 1925, Frantz teamed up with architect James Spence to form the firm of Frantz and Spence. Frantz did most of the designing while Spence handled specifications. Their partnership lasted until 1960, when they went their separate ways. Among the works of Frantz are the Saginaw Township Hall, Arthur Hill High School, the Saginaw News Building, the Montague Inn, and many schools including Potter, Morley, Chester Miller, and Handley. Frantz was active in many civic and social organizations. He was a member and president (1965) of the Saginaw Club and the Saginaw Rotary Club. He was among the first presidents of the Saginaw Art Museum, which he had remodeled when the Ring house was turned into a museum. Frantz was named a fellow of the American Institute of Architects in 1952. (Courtesy of the Castle Museum.)

Thomas McDonald Sr. was president of the Saginaw Club in 1989. He gave the toast to the office of the president in 1994 when Bill Clinton was president of the United States. McDonald was an enthusiastic booster of Saginaw. He was a leader and member of many Saginaw boards and organizations and was named Outstanding Citizen of Saginaw in 1993. (Authors' collection.)

Tom McDonald Jr. followed in his father's footsteps as president of the Saginaw Club in 1999. Thomas Jr. owns the Ford dealership in Saginaw Township. Pictured here from left to right are four McDonalds: Thomas W. Sr., Thomas W. III, Thomas J., and Thomas W. Jr. (Courtesy of Tom McDonald Jr.)

Oscar F. Wisner was one of the organizers and the first president of the East Saginaw Club. He was a lawyer and partner in the firm of Wisner and Draper. Wisner and C. Stuart Draper had offices at 125 North Washington Avenue. Wisner was vice president of the Hoyt Dry Goods Company and secretary of the James Stewart Company, wholesale grocers. (Authors' collection.)

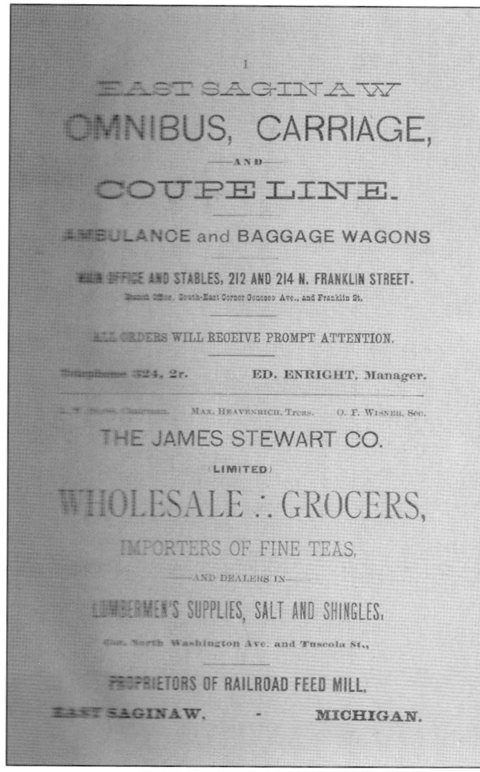

EAST SAGINAW
OMNIBUS, CARRIAGE,
—AND—
COUPE LINE.
AMBULANCE and BAGGAGE WAGONS
MAIN OFFICE AND STABLES, 212 AND 214 N. FRANKLIN STREET.
Branch Office, South-East Corner Genesee Ave., and Franklin St.
ALL ORDERS WILL RECEIVE PROMPT ATTENTION.
Telephone 324, 2r. ED. ENRIGHT, Manager.

Max. Heavenrich, Treas. O. F. Wisner, Sec.
THE JAMES STEWART CO.
(LIMITED)
WHOLESALE :. GROCERS,
IMPORTERS OF FINE TEAS,
—AND DEALERS IN—
LUMBERMEN'S SUPPLIES, SALT AND SHINGLES,
Cor. North Washington Ave. and Tuscola St.,
PROPRIETORS OF RAILROAD FEED MILL,
EAST SAGINAW. - MICHIGAN.

THE SECOND NATIONAL BANK BUILDING.
NEW HOME OF SAGINAW'S OLDEST BANKING INSTITUTION.
CAPITAL AND SURPLUS OVER $2,500,000.00

George Bidwell Morley was the East Saginaw Club's president in 1892. He was born in 1857 to John R. and Catherine Bidwell Morley in Painesville, Ohio. He moved to Saginaw in 1876 to work as a teller at Second National Bank. He became president of the bank in 1901 and chairman of the board in 1929. From 1910 to 1911, he was also a president of the Saginaw Country Club. Along with his banking work, he helped found the sugar beet industry in Saginaw. After World War I, he played a part in organizing the former Welfare League. (Courtesy of the Saginaw Country Club.)

Burrows "Buzz" Morley (1908–1989) was chairman of the board of Morley Brothers and president of the Saginaw Club in 1955. He was the son of Ralph and Lucille Burrows Morley and had three siblings, Ralph Jr., Edward B., and Julia. He was married to Julia (Kaufholtz) Morley. He gave the toast to the office of the president of the United States in 1973 when Richard Nixon was president. (Courtesy of the Saginaw Club.)

Herbert L. Ziegenbein was the Saginaw Club president during the war years of 1942–1945. He was the assistant to the division manager at Consumers Power Company. He was born on November 16, 1898, to Emil and Caroline Ziegenbein in Jackson, Michigan. He died on December 14, 1971, in Alma, Michigan. The University of Michigan received land in Gladwin County from Ziegenbein's estate that was used for oil and gas development. (Courtesy of the Saginaw Club.)

In 1881, William C. Phipps came to East Saginaw, and for a time worked as a clerk in the clothing store of "Little Jake" Seligman. Phipps later worked in the lumber camp of Eleazer Ring. In 1882, he was employed in the Wells-Stone Mercantile Company and rapidly rose in the business. In 1986, he organized the corporation of Phipps, Penoyer & Company to develop the wholesale grocery trade in the Saginaw area. He believed in the future development of Saginaw. In 1912, he was elected president of the East Saginaw Club. (Author's collection.)

William B. Mershon, the East Saginaw Club president in 1893, was a noted sportsman who traveled the country on fishing and hunting trips. He was an early conservationist who watched the indiscriminate plunder of wildlife. He wrote two books. One dealt with the passenger pigeon and the other with outdoor life. One of his favorite projects was the establishment of the Lumberman's Memorial, which stands on the high bank of the Au Sable River. (Author's collection.)

Milford Schuette, president of the Saginaw Club in 1992, was born in Saginaw. He graduated from Arthur Hill High School in 1951, graduated with honors from Michigan State University in 1958, and served in the Army during the Korean War. He became a certified public accountant as a member of the Rehmann, Robson & Company. He has been a member of the Jaycees, Kiwanis, Germania Town and Country Club, Saginaw Country Club, and the Saginaw Club for 30 years. (Courtesy of Milford Schuette.)

Giacamo "Jack" Provenzano was the club's president in 2016. He was born in 1953 in Saginaw, the third of eight children born to Dominic and Rose Provenzano. He graduated from Saginaw Valley State University and became a certified public accountant. He was a founding partner of Gardner, Provenzano & Schauman. Provenzano is a member of many civic organizations, including the Fordney Club, the Saginaw Community Foundation, and Great Lakes Bay Economics Club, among others. (Courtesy of Jack Provenzano.)

A group of former presidents posed for this photograph in 2011. From left to right are (first row) David Schooltz, unidentified, David Turner, and Michael Day; (second row) Gary Glaza, unidentified, and John Princing; (third row) David Abbs, Dr. William Scharffe, John Bintz, and Thomas McDonald Jr. (Courtesy of the Saginaw Club.)

Thomas Braley was the Saginaw Club president in 2017. He is a managing director–investment officer at Wells Fargo Advisors in Saginaw. Braley believes strongly in the value of lifelong learning. He holds the designations of certified financial planner and certified investment manager analyst and continues to pursue education opportunities that he believes will enhance his clients' well-being. He has degrees from SVSU and the University of Phoenix. He lives in a heritage home in Saginaw with his wife, Stephanie, and their four children. (Courtesy of Thomas Braley.)

Dr. William "Bill" G. Scharffe was president of the Saginaw Club in 1996. He was born and raised in Saginaw and attended Saginaw public schools, graduating from Arthur Hill High School in 1960. His father, a businessman, was also a Saginaw Club member. His mother's family owned and operated Granville Shoes Inc. in Saginaw for over 100 years. For years, Dr. Scharffe worked for the Saginaw public schools in administrative positions. He was the first public school educator to be elected president of the Saginaw Club. He served on the Saginaw City Council for 42 months, was board chairman of the Saginaw Japanese Cultural Center, is a past president of the Saginaw Exchange Club, the Michigan State alumni club of Saginaw County, and the Michigan Association of School Personnel Administrators, and is a member of many other civic organizations. Dr. Scharffe retired from Saginaw public schools in 1999 and from the Michigan Association of School Boards in 2008. He is now president and chief executive officer of Saginaw Senior Tech, a program that helps seniors with basic computer needs. He is an example of the fact that educators never really retire. (Courtesy of Dr. William Scharffe.)

# *Seven*

# Toasts to the Office of the President

Every January 1, a prominent Saginaw Club member delivers a toast to the office of the president of the United States. The first toast was delivered on New Year's Day 1913 by Judge Benton Hanchett to Pres. William Howard Taft. Thus began a tradition at the Saginaw Club. It was held for members, their sons, grandsons, and sons-in-law. In 1985, wives and daughters were invited to the ceremony. The speaker, who is chosen by the club president, remains unknown until he is introduced at noon to the gathering in the third-floor ballroom. The speech is carried on local radio stations. It was once carried on Saginaw's stations WSAM, WKNK, and WSGW. Now, it is broadcast only on WSGW. Copies of the toast are sent to the current US president, the governor of Michigan, and Michigan's members in the Senate and House of Representatives. Replies have been received and personally signed by the president or his secretary. Other replies have been received from members of Congress and Michigan's governors. Gladys Blakely, the reference librarian from the Hoyt Public Library, was working on a list of newspaper references to the toasts for club president Ralph C. Morley. She stated that after scanning the speeches, she suggested they be organized in a book for young people in the community to read. The talks should help a young person understand what was happening in America at the time of the toasts. She said the speakers were and are outstanding men in the community and represent all fields of work. The speeches were and are thought provoking, and hopefully, they are an example of cooperation in America regardless of opposing political beliefs.

The toast to the office of the president on New Year's Day 1959 was given by R. Perry Shorts, chairman of the board of Second National Bank and one of the club's oldest and most respected members. In his message, Shorts urged his audience to oppose forces that would tarnish the heritage of American freedom and private enterprise. He told the young men to be diligent in their work and honest and thrifty in their habits. He labeled inflation as one of the foremost foes of the US economy. He praised President Eisenhower for his efforts in the promotion of peace on earth, the preservation of free enterprise, and morality for the government. To the young men in attendance, he said that they did not have to be exceptionally bright to make a good living because our country is the land of opportunity. Thrift, hard work, and old-fashioned honesty are the basis of success. What one earns is not as important as what one saves. Hard work is essential, and to be honest makes for a good reputation. The economic system beats socialism by a mile. Socialism promises abundance in exchange for freedom, but those two never go together. There is never enough abundance to go around. The government has not any money to hand out to people, except what it collects in taxes from the people themselves. The welfare of the people rests on economic grounds. When business prospers, Shorts said, there is prosperity—more wealth, more factories, more goods, more jobs—and every law that hurts business hurts everybody. (Courtesy of the Castle Museum and the Saginaw Club.)

These three men were photographed at the chamber of commerce dinner on April 4, 1951. From left to right are retiring chamber president Robert H. Cook, dinner speaker Malcolm Bingay, and incoming chamber president William H. Doerfner. Both Cook and Doerfner were toast to the office of the president speakers at the Saginaw Club. (Courtesy of the Castle Museum.)

Giacamo "Jack" Provenzano gave the toast to the office of the president in 2016. His talk centered on immigration. He gave a history of his grandfather's legal immigration and work ethic. Provenzano's grandfather was a successful produce store owner who worked long hours to support his family. His advice to President Obama was to get his priorities straight—country first, political party last. Legal immigration works, and it is what keeps this country on top of the economic world. (Courtesy of Jack Provenzano.)

When Alex S. Levinsohn was a young man, he saw opportunity in the new retail automobile sales business. He sold REOs, Hudsons, and Essexes. For 35 years, he was president of the former Sutton Sales Company. For 11 years, he was president of the Saginaw Automobile Dealers Association. After his retirement in 1952, the association honored him at a testimonial dinner. He was one of the founders of Green Acres Development Company, which created the Green Acres shopping center and Green Acres Apartments. He served on the Saginaw City Council and resigned only because he moved outside of the city. His civic service included the Greater Saginaw Chamber of Commerce, Saginaw Community Chest, Advisory Board of St. Mary's Hospital, the YMCA, and the Community Clinic. In 1954, he received the Arnold Boutell Award for distinguished public service. In 1961, he gave the Saginaw Club's toast to President Eisenhower. He expressed his feelings as an American and what he considered the enduring human qualities. His talk stressed that a man must be proud of what he is, what he can do, and what he has done. Levinsohn's toast was one of the most eloquent on record. (Courtesy of the Castle Museum.)

Ellis M. Ivey Jr., general manager of Saginaw Steering Gear Division of General Motors Corporation, gave the Saginaw Club's 60th New Year's toast to the office of the president. Ivey's toast in 1972, when Richard Nixon was president, focused on the business climate. He said that American people had become critics of the free enterprise system. Many critics would seek to change the system of business ownership, which would wreck the American economy. Some had stated that American business is bilking the American consumer. The fact is that business includes everyone: government, professional men, stockholders, and all who own insurance or draw a pension. The challenge for America, he said, was to regain leadership and respect in the world. (Courtesy of the Saginaw Club.)

Daniel Fitz-Gerald, president of the Wickes Corporation, gave the toast to the office of the president in 1966. President Johnson was in office that year. Fitz-Gerald praised Johnson for his power of persuasion in keeping the steel and aluminum companies from raising their prices. Costly railroad and steel strikes were avoided after both labor and management agreed to wage contracts. (Courtesy of the Saginaw Club.)

Pres. Lyndon Johnson served the United States as president from 1963 to 1969. In 1966, he sent a congratulatory letter to Daniel Fitz-Gerald referring to Fitz-Gerald's toast to the office of the president. Johnson thanked the members of the Saginaw Club for their serious concern of important matters that impact the future of the nation. (Courtesy of the Saginaw Club.)

H. Randall Wickes remained chairman of the Wickes Corporation when Daniel Fitz-Gerald became its president. Fitz-Gerald gave the toast to the office of the president of the United States in 1966. In his talk, he mentioned that President Johnson, who took office after the assassination of President Kennedy, made a smooth transition in the government of the country. President Johnson used his power to persuade rather forceful measures in making presidential decisions. (Courtesy of the Saginaw Club.)

Dr. Francis J. McDonald gave the toast to the office of the president in 1956. A well-known dentist, his office was located in the Second National Bank Building. "Mac," as he preferred being called, was appointed to serve on the city council in 1936. He was the newest member on the council under the new council-manager government in the new city hall building. He served as mayor from 1937 to 1939. He is known to have helped school superintendent Chester F. Miller obtain federal aid for the construction of the new Arthur Hill High School. He married Mary Fordney, daughter of Congressman Joseph W. Fordney. His toast to President Eisenhower began with a prayer for the president's full recovery and praise for the Eisenhower brand of leadership, which he said gave the nation prosperity and strengthened hope for more good times and world peace. McDonald called attention to the importance of the 1956 presidential election and also made reference to the memory of the fine men who gave so much effort, time, and money to make the Saginaw Club possible. He stated that these early members were blessed with the same fine traits of character, humility, charity, ability, and integrity that current members admired in President Eisenhower. (Courtesy of the Castle Museum.)

STATE OF MICHIGAN
OFFICE OF THE GOVERNOR
LANSING

WILLIAM G. MILLIKEN
GOVERNOR

February 3, 1975

Mr. Reed T. Draper, President
Saginaw Club
219 N. Washington Avenue
Saginaw, Michigan 48607

Dear Mr. Draper:

I very much appreciated your letter of January 6 and the attachments concerning the Saginaw Club festivities on January 1.

I will read the full text with interest, and I thank you for your thoughtfulness in sending it to me.

Warm personal regards.

Sincerely,

William G. Milliken

Governor

A copy of the 1975 toast to the office of the president delivered by Robert W. Grant was sent to Pres. Gerald Ford and Michigan governor William Milliken. Both men sent responses to the Saginaw Club. Gov. William G. Milliken stated that he would read the full text of the toast with interest. The letter was personally signed. (Courtesy of the Saginaw Club.)

THE WHITE HOUSE
WASHINGTON

February 9, 1976

Dear Mr. Yeo:

Again this year I was pleased to have the opportunity to read a copy of the remarks delivered to the Saginaw Club at its annual New Year's Day meeting. Mr. James Kendrick's remarks reaffirm my faith that the spirit which built our great Nation is still very much alive. I am confident that we can look forward to America's 200th birthday with renewed hopes for peace with other countries and progress here at home.

The sentiments expressed in your toast were particularly meaningful to me. I hope you will convey my gratitude to your membership, along with my best wishes for the future.

Sincerely,

Gerald R. Ford

Mr. Lloyd J. Yeo
President
Saginaw Club
219 North Washington
Saginaw, Michigan 48607

Letters have been sent to the Saginaw Club in response to the toasts on January 1. Gerald Ford also personally signed the letter he sent referring to the toast given by James Kendrick in 1976. (Courtesy of the Saginaw Club.)

Terry Duperon, chief operating officer of Duperon Adaptive Technologies, gave an inspiring talk on January 1, 2015, in his toast to the office of the president. His speech dealt with the shifting of power as it relates to "We the People." "We, the citizens of the United States," he said, "were born to the Constitution and the Bill of Rights, and thus had power as individuals. We pay taxes so the government has money for the building of our nation, but some elected officials seem to think they allow the citizens to use the funds. But power shifts; it does not go away because someone else has it now. As for freedom of religion, it has seemed to shift to freedom from religion. Another right we have now is the right to bear arms. We have not yet given this right away and we must not. Disarming people makes them powerless. By not giving away this right, the power still is with the people. Our government's main purpose is to protect us from foreign invasion. We gave taxes for this purpose. Power shifted away from the people because we allowed the government the use of some defense money for other purposes. We traded our power for the desire to be taken care of, and by taking government hand-outs. Thus, we became dependent. If we will pull back our hands, the power will shift back to 'We the People.' " (Courtesy of Leslie Duperon.)

Burrows "Buzz" Morley gave the toast to the office of the president in 1973. He stated that Pres. Richard Nixon needed the nation's support, loyalty, and counsel in doing what was best for the country. He also praised the involvement of youth in politics and the world. He advised adults and youth to work for and nurture pride in being an American. (Courtesy of the Saginaw Club.)

Robert W. Grant gave the toast to the office of the president in 1975. He was the chairman of the Saginaw County Republican party and gave the toast to Pres. Gerald Ford. His talk stressed that individuals should participate in politics. Grant insisted that flaws in the political system are not the fault of the system but rather of the multitudes of people who prefer to watch and criticize from the sidelines. (Courtesy of the Saginaw Club.)

Prominent Saginaw attorney Robert H. Cook gave the toast to the office of the president in 1944. He emphasized support of the US president as commander in chief of the armed forces. Cook declared that Germany and Japan would destroy any government they captured and enslave their populations, making it necessary for the Allies to win the war. Enemy borders were far away, but the war covered much of the world's surface and about 90 percent of the world's population. (Authors' collection.)

William H. Doerfner, general manager of Saginaw Steering Gear Division of General Motors, gave the 52nd annual toast to the office of the president in 1964. He quoted the new president Johnson's call for renewed dedication and for united action and mutual understanding as a parallel to the future of the Saginaw community. He called for cooperation with Saginaw and its suburbs to work toward a solution for the common need for water. Doerfner called for a metropolitan look to be carriers of services and resources rather than barriers to a federation of local neighbors. (Courtesy of the Castle Museum.)

Joseph P. Day delivered the toast to the office of the president on January 1, 1992, when George Herbert Walker Bush was president. This was the 80th toast given on New Year's Day. Day's talk compared the conditions of the Saginaw community with those of the world at large. "We moved from an agriculture-based economy and a trading center to a society that was impacted by the Industrial Revolution. These changes in our society were happening as physical labor decreased and skilled labor increased. This evolution brought about an increase in the standard of living. New technologies began to change our way of life. New knowledge leads to new technologies. America has the knowledge that can shape the future of the world. Its most important asset is its people. The people with their individual and collective skills have shown great potential to their community. The business sect has responded to change by investing in employee training. Human resources are a community's most important asset. What this means for Saginaw County is that the county does not remain static. It has grown and changed because of the people who have exhibited an entrepreneurial spirit in the past. Saginaw has transitioned from an assembly-line industrial society to a people-orientated, information-driven, knowledgeable society." (Courtesy of Joseph Day.)

For many years, Dr. George Gugino practiced family medicine in Reese, Michigan. He took over his father's practice after his death in 1963. River Street in Reese has been renamed Gugino MD in honor of Dr. George Gugino and his late father, Dr. Frank Gugino, for their service to the community. In 2018, Dr. George Gugino gave the toast at the Saginaw Club to Pres. Donald Trump. His talk reflected on many of the changes that he had witnessed in the field of medicine during his years of practice. Medical notes went from hand written to electronic, and there was no Medicare or Medicaid available. The pendulum has swung over the years to very high-tech and high-cost care. Advances in medicine have been helpful to patients' care, good treatment, and well-being, but also have been very costly. Dr. Gugino discussed changes in society that he has observed such as disrespect of flag, country, and government. As for elections, he stated that Americans must learn to lose an election and compromise for the good of the country. "Let us hope the pendulum changes and Americans become American again, not a multicultural, diverse nation under socialist doctrine." (Courtesy of Dr. George Gugino.)

J. Michael Day was the speaker in 2017. His talk was given weeks before the January 20 inauguration of Donald Trump. Day mentioned the transition of power of one administration to the next, and the fact that it is one of the traditions that make our country great. He also emphasized our diverse community. Saginaw has its challenges and frustrations, but there are many in our community who work to face the challenges of those in need. Entrepreneurs need to have the freedom to do what they do best without unreasonable regulations from government. On a recent trip to Washington, DC, the Day family visited the US Senate. They listened to the Republican majority leader Mitch McConnell give a speech seeking funding to combat the spread of the Zika virus. Next, Democratic minority leader Harry Reid spoke denouncing the funding proposal for not including a variety of unrelated programs. Both speakers then left the Senate chambers. He and his family left disappointed, knowing that our representatives would rather defeat members of the opposing political party than benefit the country. (Courtesy of Michael Day.)

Hugo "Ted" Braun Jr.'s toast in 1981 was directed to president-elect Ronald Reagan. Braun stated that the significance of a new presidential administration was greater than ever before because of the election being a revolt of the American people. Reagan's election repudiated a system of ideas and governmental policies that had been in place for decades. Reagan chalked up an Electoral College landslide and a popular vote margin of some eight million. His party gained 33 seats in the House and a majority in the Senate for the first time in 26 years. The revolt was against federal programs and concepts that were not working. It was against the plunge toward national bankruptcy. The US citizens had permitted the government to chalk up budget deficits. As citizens, they had struggled with inflation, economic stagnation, and unemployment, but there had been no recession in government. Many were angry at government's solution to all social concerns—throw more dollars at the problem. People expected a return to fiscal responsibility, with tough measures against inflation, based upon a balanced budget. People expected a government that recognizes that the best social program is a job. "Let us be ever mindful of the people's role in achieving success. Let them accept their responsibilities with the same enthusiasm with which they demand their rights." (Courtesy of Ruth Braun.)

The speaker selected to give the toast to the office of the president of the United States in 1992 was Milford Schuette. Schuette was a certified public accountant and a partner with Rehmann, Robson & Company. He noted that the Saginaw Club was departing from a tradition that had limited attendance at the toasts to members, their sons, and grandsons. The club now allowed wives, daughters, and granddaughters of members to attend. In his toast to Pres. Ronald Reagan, Schuette pointed to the federal deficit and taxes as the nation's most pressing problems. Referring to the budget, Schuette stated that across the board line-item slashes are not always the most desirable because of the effects on an expanding economy, but waste management and the elimination of ineffective government programs were to be desired. He stated, "The defense budget could be trimmed by more than 10 percent by allowing private enterprise to compete with less government interference. If private enterprise were to manage waste control we would get results at no sacrifice to our weapons program, to our military personnel or our space projects." (Courtesy of Milford Schuette.)

Milford Schuette gave the toast to the office of the president in 1985. In his talk, he stressed the nation's problems of taxes and the deficit. Ronald Reagan was president. (Courtesy of Milford Schuette.)

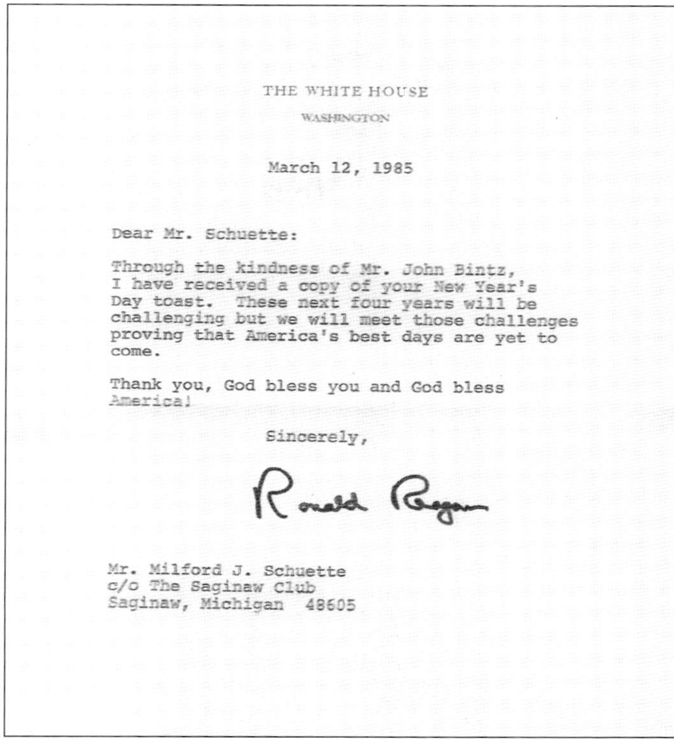

THE WHITE HOUSE

WASHINGTON

March 12, 1985

Dear Mr. Schuette:

Through the kindness of Mr. John Bintz, I have received a copy of your New Year's Day toast. These next four years will be challenging but we will meet those challenges proving that America's best days are yet to come.

Thank you, God bless you and God bless America!

Sincerely,

Ronald Reagan

Mr. Milford J. Schuette
c/o The Saginaw Club
Saginaw, Michigan 48605

Ronald Reagan was the 40th president of the United States in 1985. He sent a letter to the Saginaw Club in response to Milford Schuette's toast to the office of the president on January 1. (Courtesy of the Saginaw Club.)

Thomas Basil Jr. delivered the 106th toast on January 1, 2019. Basil began his remarks with the reason the tradition of the toast began: "On January 1, 1913, Benton Hanchett had a good friend named William Howard Taft. Taft happened to be the 27th president of the United States, but two months earlier, he lost his second term as president to Woodrow Wilson. Some historians believe that Taft was in attendance at the East Saginaw Club when Hanchett gave the first toast. Others claim that Taft visited the club the following year as an ex-president. What is certain is that William Howard Taft is one of the many celebrities who have set foot in the Saginaw Club. The tradition of the toast provides a sense of community and what it means to be an American. Sometimes, US citizens take their freedoms and successful system of government for granted, forgetting the hardships of citizens who came before. On January 1, club members and their guests toast to freedom and those who gave it. Freedom is not free; it was bought at a high price. May the office of the president be guided by wisdom, protection of our freedoms, and the safety of US shores. May the office be an example to the American people, and may the Saginaw Club tradition help unite the community and the nation for the next 106 years." (Courtesy of Thomas Basil.)

Robert W. Grant, president of Grant Grocers, gave the toast to the office of the president in 1975. He urged his audience to join in voluntary participation in politics beginning at the county level. Grant and his wife, Patricia, donated a gift to Delta College in support of the arts and humanities. Their endowment established two scholarships annually to Saginaw students who study art at Delta College. (Courtesy of Delta College.)

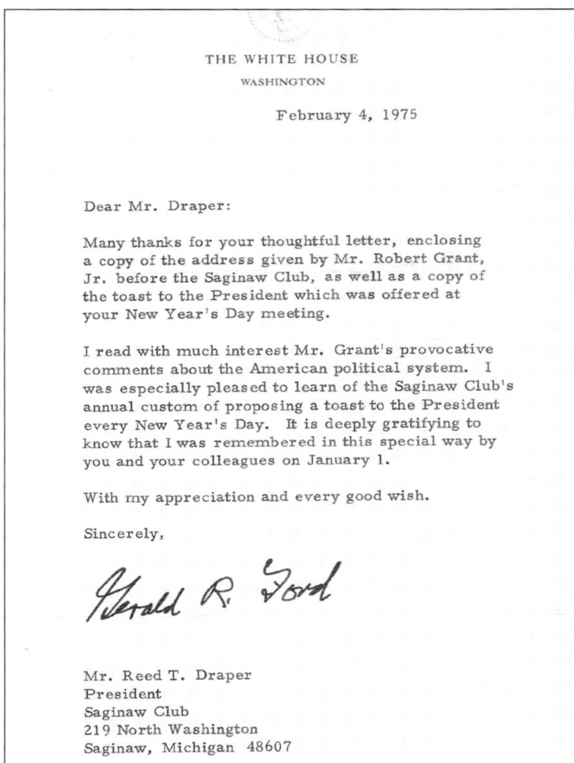

THE WHITE HOUSE
WASHINGTON

February 4, 1975

Dear Mr. Draper:

Many thanks for your thoughtful letter, enclosing a copy of the address given by Mr. Robert Grant, Jr. before the Saginaw Club, as well as a copy of the toast to the President which was offered at your New Year's Day meeting.

I read with much interest Mr. Grant's provocative comments about the American political system. I was especially pleased to learn of the Saginaw Club's annual custom of proposing a toast to the President every New Year's Day. It is deeply gratifying to know that I was remembered in this special way by you and your colleagues on January 1.

With my appreciation and every good wish.

Sincerely,

Gerald R. Ford

Mr. Reed T. Draper
President
Saginaw Club
219 North Washington
Saginaw, Michigan 48607

This is a letter sent to the Saginaw Club referring to Robert Grant's toast to the office of the president. It was signed by then president Gerald R. Ford. (Courtesy of the Saginaw Club.)

Harold D. Draper gave the toast to the office of the president in 1963. Pictured here are early images of Draper. He was prominent for years in the automobile sales and financing field. There were 260 people in attendance for this 51st toast. Draper's entire talk was an eloquent prayer that America be guided and led by the principles that suit its greatness. He stressed that Americans be reminded of the privileges of parenthood—to train children with educational facilities to give them the intellect and training to carry on successfully in the complex life of the future—to teach them love of God and devotion to country. (Courtesy of the Saginaw Club.)

Following the club tradition, which first began in 1913, club president Kenneth "Mac" MacDonald introduced the 2013 toastmaster, Herbert Spence III. Radio station WSGW carries the broadcast each year. Shown here is the station's announcer Art Lewis (left) with MacDonald. (Courtesy of the Saginaw Club.)

The toastmaster in 2013 was Herb Spence III. Spence has a very distinguished biography dating back to his graduation with an engineering degree from the University of Michigan. Spence, with a decidedly conservative tone to his toast, highlighted three important qualities for effective leaders: communication, collaboration, and courage. (Courtesy of the Saginaw Club.)

# INDEX